Help a Friend Recover

A Practical Guide — What to Say, What to Do, and How to Set Boundaries

Gearóid Carey

Copyright © 2025 Gearóid Carey

Published 2025.

All rights reserved.

This book and its content are protected by copyright law. Therefore, no part of this book may be reproduced or used in any form without the explicit written permission of the author, except as permitted by copyright law, such as limited copying for educational purposes or brief quotations in reviews.

Disclaimer

This book is intended for educational and supportive purposes only.

It is not a substitute for professional medical, psychological, psychiatric, or crisis care. The ideas, tools, and examples shared here are designed to help you think more clearly, respond more compassionately, and support someone more effectively – not to diagnose, treat, or replace professional services.

Everyone's situation is different. Recovery looks different for each person, and what feels helpful in one context may not be appropriate in another. Always use your judgement, stay within your own limits, and prioritise safety – both theirs and yours.

If the person you care about is at risk of harm, experiencing a medical or mental-health emergency, or in immediate danger, seek urgent professional help through local emergency services, crisis lines, or qualified healthcare providers.

This book encourages reflection, learning, and informed support – but responsibility for decisions and actions remains with the reader. The author accepts no liability for how the information in this book is used or interpreted.

Most importantly: You are not expected to do this alone. When in doubt, reach out for professional guidance and support.

Contents

Who This Book Is For	VII
How to Use This Book	IX
1. Be Safe and Be Well	1
2. Help Them Build Strengths, Supports and Resources	21
3. Help Them Measure Progress	52
4. Help Them Learn New Skills	75
5. Advice from 20 Years of Experience	183
6. Enabling, Crisis, and Critical Situations — How to Respond Well	194
7. Dealing with Guilt, Shame, and Regret	222
8. Be Honest, Genuine and Truthful	228
9. What If They Don't Want to Change?	237

10. The Greatest Secret of Recovery	266
Ongoing Support & Next Steps	270
About the Author	271
Discover More Books	272

Who This Book Is For

This book is for anyone who cares deeply about someone who is struggling – whether it's addiction, mental health challenges, trauma, loss, or a crisis that has turned life upside down.

It's for friends who feel helpless, parents who lie awake worrying, partners who don't know what to say anymore, and family members walking on eggshells trying not to make things worse.

Maybe you're not personally affected, but you want to be there for someone you care about – or maybe you're worn out, confused, and overwhelmed by advice that never seems to help. Either way, this book is here for you.

GEARÓID CAREY

If you've ever thought *"I don't know what to do"* or *"I'm afraid I'll say the wrong thing"* then this book was written for you.

You're not alone.

And there is a way forward.

How to Use This Book

This book is designed to be simple, practical, and easy to use – **no experience needed**. If you're brand new to recovery, it will get you up to speed quickly. If you already have experience, it will provide invaluable tips and tools to help you support someone more effectively.

Each chapter focuses on what actually helps – what to say, what not to say, what to do, and how to set healthy boundaries without losing yourself in the process.

You'll find:

- **Clear guidance** on how to support someone through addiction, mental health crises, trauma, grief, or major life challenges.

- **Examples of real conversations** to help you understand what supportive communication looks and sounds like.

- **Simple tools and strategies** you can use immediately, even in the middle of chaos.

- **Short reflection questions** to help you think about your situation and decide what's right for you.

- **Practical steps** for protecting your own wellbeing while helping someone you care about.

Take what you need. Skip what you don't. Come back to it whenever you feel lost, unsure, or in need of strength.

You don't have to do this perfectly – you just have to care, be genuine, and stay open to reflecting and learning as you go.

Chapter One

Be Safe and Be Well

In this chapter, you'll learn how to support someone in crisis without losing yourself. The key is awareness.

Are you safe?

Are you well?

It isn't easy, and no one can do it perfectly. But we can do it well enough – to be there for them now, and over the long haul if needed.

When someone we care about is struggling – whether it's addiction, depression, anxiety, trauma, or a crisis that's turned their world upside down – it's natural to want to throw ourselves into helping them. And we do it from love. We do it because they matter to us. We do it because we'd give anything to see them well again.

But here's the truth most people don't realise until they're already exhausted:

You cannot help someone effectively if you lose yourself in the process.

To support someone else through a difficult time, you must have two foundations in place:

    1. Be Safe.

    2. Be Well.

These two rules are simple, but they are powerful. They create the solid ground you need beneath your feet so you don't get swept away by someone else's storm.

Be Safe

Being safe means protecting the parts of your life that matter – your emotional safety, your mental wellbeing, your physical safety, your time, your finances, and even your personal space.

And this is different for everyone.

For some, personal safety might mean not being shouted at or manipulated.
For others, it might mean not handing over money that puts your bills at risk.
For some, it could be meeting in public places if someone is unpredictable, intoxicated, or volatile.
For many, it means boundaries–knowing when to step back, when to say *not now*, and when to say *enough*.

Sometimes safety won't feel like a problem at all. Everything might feel calm and manageable, and that's wonderful. But life changes fast, and crises can escalate quickly–so it's wise to review this regularly and keep an eye on it.

And sometimes – because our love is fierce – we might choose to stretch beyond what's comfortable. We do it willingly, because our hearts insist on it. And that's okay. There is no judgement here. Only honesty.

Just remember: **if you burn yourself out completely, you won't be able to help anyone—not now, not later on.**

Protecting your own safety doesn't mean abandoning someone you care about.
It means staying strong enough to stay *with* them.

Give yourself permission to be safe.
Give yourself permission to protect your boundaries.
Give yourself permission to matter too.

Be Well

The second part is caring for *your* life—your emotional needs, your physical health, your sleep, your friendships, your work, your joy.

Supporting someone through crisis can be heavy.
It can take over your world without you even noticing it happening.
Days become centred around their needs.
Your needs slide quietly into the background.

That's when exhaustion creeps in.
That's when resentment or hopelessness quietly take hold.
That's when your capacity to help begins to shrink.

Being well is an act of love – both for them and for you.

Eat. Rest. Exercise. Laugh. Have time off. Keep living your life.
Do the things that make you feel like yourself.

The healthier and stronger you are, the more resourceful, patient, and present you can be when you sit across from someone in pain – not just for today, but for the long run.

You are not selfish for taking care of yourself.
You are preparing yourself to help better.

Professional Wisdom, Personal Application

In my professional work, these two rules—*be safe and be well*—are non-negotiable.

We frequently talk about risks, policies, meeting locations, and safety planning. We think ahead. We ask *what might be wise here?* We review concerns regularly, not because we expect disaster, but because preparation keeps everyone safe.

And the same principles apply to you personally.
If you're meeting someone using heavy drugs, meet in a public place during the day.
If emotions run high, have support for yourself.
If something feels unsafe, trust that feeling.
Talk with trusted friends. Review as you go. Adjust when needed.

Professionally, if I am well – rested, supported, balanced – then I am able to be present and helpful.
Personally, the same truth holds: **your strength, your steadiness, is the greatest gift you can offer.**

Support looks different when it's a friend, a partner, a child, or a sibling, of course. The heart is involved. The stakes are high. But the core principles are universal:

Be safe.
Be well.
You'll help more effectively when you are standing on solid ground.

Coming Up Next

In the next chapter, we'll explore how to help someone build their strengths, supports, and resources – the foundations that make recovery possible.

After that, we'll look at how to help them measure their progress, because knowing whether things are actually changing – improving, worsening, or staying stuck – removes confusion, eases anxiety, and gives a clear sense of direction.

But none of that works well unless you start here:

Protect yourself.
Care for yourself.
Connect with support for yourself.

Because the world needs you steady, loving, and whole – not unsure and exhausted beside the person you're trying to help. In the following chapters I'll show you how to help people recover – so you can feel confident you are doing the right things.

> **Key Reminder**
>
> You are allowed to take care of yourself while supporting someone you love.
>
> It's not selfish. It's essential.

Reflection Exercise: Your Safety & Wellness Check-In

Take a quiet moment now. Breathe, and let your mind settle. Read the questions that follow with no rush and no pressure. Just sit with them for now. We'll come back to them later in the chapter.

There are no right or wrong answers – only honesty, and the quiet clarity that arrives when you allow yourself to pause.

1. Where am I currently feeling safe in this relationship?
What about it feels steady, manageable or grounded?

2. Where do I feel unsafe or uneasy – emotionally, physically, financially, or in terms of my time and energy?
What parts of my life feel at risk or stretched?

3. What boundaries might help protect my wellbeing?
What do I need to say "No" to? What do I need to limit?

4. What would taking care of myself look like this week?
Think of one small action for your physical wellbeing
Think of one small action for your emotional wellbeing.
Think of one small action for your daily life or routine.

5. Who can support *me* in this?
Name one person you could talk to openly.

When you're finished, place a hand on your chest and say quietly:

I matter too. I am allowed to take care of myself.

Key Points to Remember

A simple, practical summary of this chapter

- **You cannot help someone effectively if you lose yourself in the process.**

- **Being safe** means protecting your emotional, physical, financial, and personal boundaries.

- Safety looks different for every person and every situation – review it regularly.

- **Being well** means continuing to care for your own life, needs, and wellbeing.

- When you stay grounded, rested, and strong, you support more effectively.

- It is not selfish to look after yourself – it is wise, necessary, and loving.

- You can love someone deeply *and* protect yourself at the same time.

> - Supporting someone is often a marathon, not a sprint – pace yourself and protect your strength for the long haul.

A Story to Bring This Home

Let me tell you about Aoife.

Aoife's younger brother, Cian, fell into addiction. For months, she tried everything to help him. She answered every late-night call, spent money she didn't have, missed work, cancelled plans, and carried the weight of his pain on her shoulders. She barely slept. She cried in the car before going into work. Still, she kept giving, believing that if she just gave a little more, it might be the thing that finally saved him.

One night, she drove at 2 a.m. to pick him up from a dangerous estate where he'd been robbed and beaten. When she got home, shaking and exhausted, she realised she couldn't go on like this.

The next morning she sat with her coffee and whispered to herself, *"If I break, I'm no use to anyone. Not even him."*

So she changed her approach.

- She still loved him. She still showed up. But she set boundaries:
- She stopped giving money.
- She only met him during the day, in public places.
- She kept her routine–exercise, sleep, meals, work.
- She let other family members share the load.
- She refused to answer calls during the night.

At first, she felt guilty. But something powerful happened.

When she became steady, calm, and well, she was suddenly far more helpful. Her voice was clearer. Her boundaries were respected. And slowly, Cian began to stabilise – not because she saved him, but because she consistently offered hope, understanding, support, and practical guidance. She was an anchor in his chaos.

Years later, Cian is in recovery. And when he looks back, he doesn't say, *"You should have done more."*

He says, *"Thank you for staying strong when I couldn't."*

Final Thought

Being safe and being well is not abandoning someone. It's staying strong enough to walk beside them all the way.

Later in the book, we'll talk about something that removes confusion and gives real peace of mind: **how to measure progress** – so you can know what's working, what isn't, and when things are changing.

For now, breathe. You're doing better than you think.

> For the One Who Cares
>
> Hold steady, dear heart.
> You're not meant to drown
> in someone else's storm.
> Anchor yourself.
> Breathe.
> Stand tall.

GEARÓID CAREY

Love is not measured
by how much you sacrifice,
but by how strongly you can stand
and still offer your hand.
Walk beside them –
not in front, not behind.
Be a steady companion.
Together, find the way.
Forward, one step at a time.

Journal Worksheet & Reflection Pages

Use this space for honest reflection. Be gentle with yourself.

1. What parts of my life currently feel safe and steady?
Where am I grounded and supported?

_____

_____

_____

2. What areas feel unsafe, stretched, or overwhelming?
Emotionally, physically, financially, in time or energy.

_____

_____

_____

3. What boundary could support my wellbeing right now?
What do I need to protect or limit?

_____

_____

4. What is one small action I'll take this week to care for myself?
Body / emotions / routine / connection / rest

_____

_____

_____

5. Who can support me while I support someone else?
A friend, a sibling, a parent, a professional, a group

_____

_____

_____

Now, place a hand on your heart again and say:
"I matter too. Looking after myself is an act of strength."

Weekly Check-In

1. **How safe do I feel? (0–10)**

2. **How well am I caring for myself? (0–10)**

If the score is below 8, think about making some changes. If it is 5 or below, make plans to improve it over the next week.

If the score is below 8 – consider small changes

Examples (Safety):

- **Reach out to someone you trust.**
  A conversation with a friend, partner, or colleague can help you feel more grounded, less alone, and give you the perspective you need to set necessary boundaries for your safety.

- **Reduce contact with stressful situations.**
  If certain people, places, or online spaces make you uneasy, step back a little this week.

- **Strengthen your daily routine.**
  Simple things – locking doors, keeping your

phone charged, planning your day, letting someone know where you are and when you plan to be back – can increase your sense of safety.

Examples (Self-Care):

- **Add one nourishing habit.**
  A 10-minute walk, a proper breakfast, or getting to bed 30 minutes earlier can help lift your self-care score.

- **Ease off on something draining.**
  Cut back on scrolling, reduce late-night work, or give yourself permission to cancel a non-essential commitment.

- **Reach for comfort, not perfection.**
  Make a warm meal, tidy one corner of the room, or take a long shower – small acts build momentum.

If the score is 5 or below – make a clear plan for the week ahead

Examples (Safety):

- **Tell someone you're struggling and ask for support.**
  Let a trusted person know you don't feel safe – this is a strength, not a weakness. Work as a team to support the person you all care about.

- **Plan ahead to protect yourself if a situation might be harmful or become unstable.**
  Bring a friend, choose public spaces, and give yourself permission to leave at any point if it doesn't feel safe.

- **Create a simple safety plan.**
  Write down who to call, where to go, and what steps to take if your sense of safety drops suddenly.

Examples (Self-Care)

- **Plan your week around essentials.**
  Sleep, meals, rest, short walks – schedule them the same way you would schedule an appointment.

- **Ask for practical help.**

This might mean childcare, a lift to the shops, help preparing meals, or delegating tasks at work. Sometimes we forget that there are people there who want to help, and we don't have to go it alone.

- **Book one supportive appointment.**
  There are support groups for people supporting someone in recovery – try one out. And consider making an appointment with a GP, a counsellor, or a professional who works in this field for some advice and guidance.

A Gentle Reminder

You cannot pour from an empty cup.
Refilling yourself is not shameful – it's sacred.

Chapter Two

Help Them Build Strengths, Supports and Resources

When someone we care about is struggling, it's natural to want to fix things – to find the right words, the right advice, the right solution. But recovery doesn't usually work like that. What actually helps someone recover is far simpler – and far more powerful: **as they gradually build strengths, supports, and resources, healing begins.**

Let's break this down using a few comparison vignettes.

Two People, Same Struggle – Very Different Outcomes

Imagine two people: Jane and Joe.

Both are going through a deeply difficult period in life. They're struggling to function in important areas – work, social life, relationships. Their internal wellbeing is low. They feel overwhelmed, disconnected, and worn down.

At this point, to understand how healing works, the cause isn't the focus. It may be a mental-health relapse, a first episode of severe distress, addiction, trauma, loss or bereavement – or a combination of these.

What matters is this: both Jane and Joe are struggling badly.

Now let's look a little closer at their situations.

Jane has a friend she talks to twice a week – once on the phone and once over coffee. She feels she can confide in this person. She has a park nearby and goes for a walk most mornings, even on hard days. She's connected with a counsellor. She's read a few books that help her make sense of what's happening. And she's using a simple tool to track how she's doing week to week.

Joe, on the other hand, keeps to himself. He doesn't feel there's anyone he can really talk to. He doesn't have places he feels comfortable going. He isn't connected with professional support. He doesn't understand what's happening to him. He's just trying to get through each day.

So let me ask you:

Who is more likely to recover?
Who is likely to stabilise sooner?
Who is more at risk of staying stuck?

The answer is obvious.

Recovery Capital – The Ingredient That Makes the Difference

What Jane has – and Joe doesn't – is something called **recovery capital**.

Recovery capital is simply the **sum of the strengths, supports, and resources** a person can draw on during a difficult time.

Decades of research across mental health, addiction, and trauma recovery consistently point to the same conclusion:

> People with higher recovery capital recover more quickly, more sustainably, and with fewer relapses.

That probably feels like common sense – but it matters, because it tells us *where to focus our energy.*

Recovery isn't driven by willpower alone. It's driven by what someone has around them – and within them – to support change.

Why Engagement Matters More Than "Having" Support

Now here's the part the research also makes very clear – and it's crucial.

It's not just *having* recovery capital that matters.
It's **how it feels to engage with it**.

Let me show you what I mean.

Meet Brenda and Billy. On paper, they look identical.

Both have:

- a friend who says, "Call me anytime,"
- a nearby park they walk in regularly,
- a counsellor they see weekly,
- recovery-related books they've read,
- and a self-tracking tool.

Same supports. Same resources.

But their experience is very different.

Brenda doesn't really feel comfortable talking to her friend. Their conversations stay surface-level. She goes to the park, but doesn't feel safe there. She sees the counsellor, but doesn't feel understood, and the worksheets don't connect. She's read some books, but they didn't really inspire her. The tracking tool feels flat and meaningless.

Billy, on the other hand, feels genuinely supported. He trusts his friend and opens up to him. He finds walks in the park helpful – even on bad days, they offer a little comfort. He feels understood by his counsellor and uses the worksheets as homework during the week. The books he's read really speak to him. The tracking tool feels helpful and motivating.

Now ask yourself again: *Who is going to do better?*

The Multiplier Effect: Why a Person's Experience of Support Matters So Much

Let's use a simple illustration.

Imagine both Brenda and Billy have five "units" of recovery capital – as listed above.

On paper, they look the same.

But Brenda's experience of that support is poor. It doesn't feel safe, meaningful, or engaging. So its *real impact* is maybe only **10%**.

Five units × 10% = **0.5 effective units**

Billy's experience is positive and meaningful. His engagement amplifies the impact, let's say ten times.

Five units × 10 = **50 effective units**

Same supports.

Wildly different outcomes.

This is why forcing support rarely works – and why helping someone find what fits them is so powerful. When support feels safe, meaningful, and is a good fit for the person, its impact grows far beyond what it looks like on paper. What matters most is not the support itself, but how it's experienced.

> **The lesson is simple:**
>
> It's not just how much recovery capital a person has, but how they experience it that makes all the difference.

When people feel accepted, understood, inspired, and appropriately challenged, there's a kind of magic in the air – a quiet tingle of optimism, balanced by realism.

Four decades of research underline a simple idea: a person's subjective experience of the people and resources they connect with has a powerful impact on outcomes.

The Three Areas That Matter Most

To keep this simple, recovery capital can be grouped into three areas:

1. **Strengths**

    Internal resources – skills, insight, confidence, routines, and coping strategies.

2. **Support**

    People they feel understood and accepted by – and who are willing to help: friends, family, peers, and professionals.

3. **Resources**

    Tools, services, community groups, books, and information – anything that doesn't fit into the first two categories.

So, in one sentence, here's how to help a friend recover:

> *Your role is to help them build their strengths, supports, and resources – their recovery capital – in a way that feels right and meaningful to them.*

That's it. Take a moment here. Breathe. Reflect. Maybe go for a little walk and let that sentence settle. This is the key. And once you truly get it, you'll come back to it again and again as you walk alongside your friend, family member, or loved one on their path of recovery: *How can I help them build their strengths, supports, and resources in a way that's meaningful to them?*

What *You* Can Do (And It Matters More Than You Think)

The fact that you're reading this book means you're already part of their recovery capital. Now let's look at how to **amplify your impact** using what we've learned so far.

Start with this fundamental truth:

Simply by being there – listening, checking in, and offering a steady presence – you are already making a difference.

You don't need the perfect words.
You don't need all the answers.

Your consistency, care, and willingness to stay connected matter more than you realise.

You can:

- Sit with them.
- Listen.
- Let them know you're always just on the other end of the phone.
- Ask how you can help – and if it's reasonable, do it.
- Send a text once a week, or more often if it feels right.
- Ask if they feel up for a walk or a coffee.
- Share ideas gently.
- Explore options together.
- Suggest supports, and offer to help them connect if that feels helpful.
- Encourage small experiments – new routines or

new ways of looking at things – and talk about how it went.

- Help them reflect on what feels helpful and what doesn't.

- Listen to what they're learning about their journey.

- Encourage them to explore their own ideas about change and what they might try next.

You might say:

- "Do you want to go for a coffee and have a chat?"

- "You're always welcome to come round if you're feeling low and want some company – we could listen to music, watch a movie, or just have a cuppa."

- "Have you thought about seeing a GP or a counsellor?"

- "There's a class, group, or park nearby – would you like to check it out together?"

- "Let's look at a few books and see if any ideas stand out as helpful."

The key is how they experience these offers of support. Don't be frustrated – be patient. Accept where they are, and remember that every small step matters. Match their pace. Don't overwhelm them with options or ideas. What may seem like a small step to you can be a very big step in their recovery.

You're not fixing them. You're adding. And each small thing you add brings recovery a little closer.

And if possible, don't support them alone. Often there are others who want to help too. Remember, you're there for each other as well. You can share ideas and offer one another emotional support. Let your friend or family member know that there is a team around them – people who care, who wish them well, and who are walking alongside them.

Progress Is Built – Not Magically Achieved

Recovery usually doesn't arrive all at once.

It shows up as:

- One more support than last week

- One small routine added

- One insight discovered

- One small refinement to the plan

- One point higher on the tracker

Some weeks things won't improve – and that's okay.

Some weeks things may even get worse – and that's okay too.

Your steadiness, patience, and belief matter – especially when change feels slow.

But trust me, this approach to recovery works. As the ingredients that drive change are added, meaningful improvement begins to show – often week by week.

A Final Sprinkle of Research (And Why It's Encouraging)

Across decades of outcome research in mental health, addiction, and trauma recovery, the same pattern shows up again and again. Regardless of the approach used, **four factors consistently predict improvement**:

- **Hope and expectancy** (~15%)
  A belief – even a fragile one – that things can get better.

- **Supportive relationships** (~30%)
  Feeling understood, accepted, and not alone in the struggle.

- **Structure and plan** (~15%)
  Having some kind of direction, routine, or agreed way of working through things.

- **Personal strengths and resources**
  The person's own abilities, insights, interests, coping skills, and inner drive – often the largest contributor of all, accounting for between 40 and 87 percent of the outcome.

These percentages aren't meant to be exact or technical. They're a guide.

They're make one simple point:

Change doesn't come from one perfect intervention. It comes from a combination of these ingredients working together.

Now notice something important.

You can influence **every single one of these**.

When you show up with patience and belief, you help build hope.
When you listen without judgement, you strengthen relationships.
When you help create a simple plan or routine, you add structure.
And when you encourage their ideas, recognise their strengths, and trust their experience, you help them connect with their own internal resources – their strengths.

You don't need special training to do this.
You don't need to get it right every time.

By being steady, kind, and curious – by walking alongside rather than trying to rescue – you're already contributing to the very factors that drive recovery.

By giving them the gift of your time, the wisdom of your counsel, and the radiance of your heart, you are making a difference – nurturing the very factors that create change.

That's why your role matters far more than you might realise.

The Simple Formula

Here it is, distilled:

> Help them build their strengths, supports, and resources in ways that feel meaningful, safe, and engaging to them.
>
> *As recovery capital grows, healing follows.*

And you – patiently, steadily – are part of that process. Bringing a quiet confidence, trusting the process, knowing how healing unfolds.

Remember this:
You don't have to save them.

You just have to walk beside them – and help them gather what they need to heal.

In the next chapter, I'll show you how to help someone measure their progress. Measuring progress helps people see when things are improving, when they're stuck, and when they may be getting worse. It adds a sense of clarity and control to the recovery process, empowering people to find the path forward that's right for them. It's a powerful way to be an ally – reflecting together on their chart, talking through how things have been going, and creating space to think about the path ahead.

Key Points to Remember from this Chapter:

- **As recovery capital grows, healing follows.**
  People recover as their strengths, supports, and resources grow.

- **How support is experienced matters a lot.**
  Support that feels safe, meaningful, and like a good fit has the greatest impact.

- **Small steps matter** – especially at the beginning.

- You don't need perfect words or all the answers; **steady presence, commitment and healthy boundaries** are what they need most from you.

- **You're not rescuing – you're adding.**
  This is a breakthrough paradigm shift – a powerful change in mindset that unlocks your ability to help someone heal.

- **You don't have to do this alone.** Connect with others who can support you as you help – professionals, concerned-others groups, family members, and friends.

Reflections

Take a few quiet moments to reflect on these questions. There's no rush, and no right or wrong answers.

- Where do I naturally *add* support, rather than try to fix?

- What strengths, supports, or resources does my friend already have – even in small ways?

- How does the support I offer *feel* from their point of view?

- Am I matching their pace, or unintentionally pushing my own?

- What is one small, realistic way I could add to their recovery capital this week?

You don't need to answer all of these. One honest reflection is powerful enough to move things forward.

A Short Pause

Take a moment now.

Breathe in slowly.
Breathe out gently.

Let your shoulders drop.
Let the urgency soften.

You are not responsible for the whole journey.
You are walking beside them – not carrying them.

Notice what it feels like to hold steady presence without pressure.
This is often where the deepest support lives.

You know how this works now.

You're ready to help – to nurture healing.

Guiding Wisdoms (For When You Feel Frustrated or Drained)

What seems like a small step to you may feel like the first ray of hope to them.

What feels like "not enough" to you may feel like progress to them.

What feels ordinary to you may feel stabilising to them.

What feels like standing still to you may feel like holding on for them.

What feels silent to you may feel peaceful to them.

Sometimes we can't change much about the situation today, but we can let the person know they're not alone – and that can change everything.

You don't need to see the whole path – just find the next step together.

Worksheet 1: Your Role as Support (Grounding the Mindset)

Purpose:
To anchor you in the "not rescuing – adding" paradigm.

Instructions:
Take a few quiet minutes. Write short, honest answers. One or two lines is enough.

Complete the sentences:

I feel most helpful when I am

_____

_____

_____

I sometimes feel pressure to "fix" things when

_____

When I remind myself that I'm adding, not rescuing, I feel

Reflection:

What does walking beside them look like in practice for me right now?

Worksheet 2: Recovery Capital Map (Seeing What's Already There)

Purpose:
To help you notice existing strengths and opportunities, instead of focusing only on what's missing.

Personal Strengths (Internal Resources)
List any strengths you already see – even small ones.

_____

_____

_____

Supports (People)
Who feels even somewhat safe or supportive to them?

_____

_____

Resources (Tools, Activities, Groups and Online Resources)

Anything that helps, grounds, or stabilises – even slightly.

Reflection:

Which one feels most meaningful to them right now?

Worksheet 3: Adding Without Overwhelming

Purpose:
To encourage small, realistic contributions.

This week, I might add ONE small thing by:

☐ Checking in with a message

☐ Offering time together

☐ Listening, and limiting myself to only offering one piece of advise or guidance (choosing it carefully)

☐ Exploring a new option together

☐ Asking what they feel they need right now

☐ Asking what they feel they need right now

Challenge yourself to grow in your ability to support them.
Write down one new thing you'll contribute this week:

Check-in question to ask myself:
How do I think they will feel about this, and how will they experience it?

You don't have to be a mind reader. You can suggest something and simply ask how they feel about it. If they feel it's a good step, you can move forward together. If they have concerns, talk them through. You can always choose a different step for this week – and come back to this one in the future.

Or maybe it just wasn't a useful idea – and that's okay. I can't count how many times I've suggested something to a client and, after talking it through, we've both realised it wasn't the right fit – and even had a laugh about it. Sometimes I'll say, "Yes, that was a really bad idea I suggested."

And that's okay. We're both human, and doing our best is enough. We simply let it go and move on – glad we were open enough to explore the option, and wise enough to recognise that there were better ones.

Worksheet 4: When You Feel Frustrated or Drained

Purpose:
To support the supporter.

Circle the idea that help you most today:

- Small steps matter.

- Presence is enough.

- I don't have to carry this alone.

- What feels slow may be safely paced.

- I'm allowed to rest too.

Write one sentence you want to remember this week:

_____

_____

Who can support you right now?

___

___

___

> **Remember:**
> You don't have to save them.
> You're not failing if things move slowly.
> You're adding – and that matters.

Chapter Three

Help Them Measure Progress

When someone is going through a tough time – mental-health struggles, addiction, trauma, overwhelming grief, or a major life upheaval – it can be hard for them to see how they're really doing. Some days blur together. Some weeks feel lost. That's why measuring progress, compassionately and simply, can be life-changing.

Here's a short set of weekly questions you can use together. They're not for diagnosing anyone. They're for sparking helpful conversations, noticing changes, and finding ways to make next week a little easier than the last.

The Five Weekly Questions

Thinking about the past week...

1. **How did you do at connecting with positive and supportive people?**
   Not so good – OK – Good

2. **How were things in your close relationships?**
   Difficult – Not so good – OK

3. **How were things socially – at work, school, college, out shopping, at events, or groups you normally attend?**
   Difficult – Not so good – OK

4. **How were your emotions and feelings?**
   Difficult – Not so good – OK

5. **Overall, how was your week?**
   Difficult – Not so good – OK

Each option is scored as: 0 = first option, 1 = second, 2 = third.

So the total score goes from 0 to 10.

- 8–10: Doing fairly well – still worth talking through the week.

- 5–7: Concerning – something is affecting wellbeing.

- 0–4: Very concerning – the person is likely struggling.

But remember: this is not about labels or diagnoses. It's about opening up a meaningful conversation and finding ways to help them feel even *one point* better next week. And half points absolutely count. If someone feels they're between Not so good and OK, the score is 1.5. You'd be surprised how often a half-point feels exactly right – and how validating it is to actually see that progress.

If They're Struggling to Answer

If they can't quite find their footing with a question, just add the word "Overall" at the beginning.

For example: *"Overall, how were your emotions and feelings over the past week?"*

That one word helps people zoom out and look at the bigger picture.

Why These Questions Work

Here's the fascinating thing: when someone is in a period of deep distress, all the scores tend to drop together. And as they recover, those same scores rise together. That's why the total score is such a clear indicator of progress.

Recovery isn't a subtle shift. It's the difference between barely functioning and being able to live again. It's a bit like the difference between a car that won't start and a car that's back on the road – not subtle at all. And that's another reason why the total score from these questions is such a good representation of change.

Or, if we want the more technical phrasing: **these questions have strong psychometric properties.** They're reliable indicators of whether someone is experiencing deep distress and how their recovery is unfolding over time. That's enough technical talk for this book – if you're curious, I explore all of this in much more detail in my other books.

The First Question: A Window Into Their Recovery Process

"How did you do at connecting with positive and supportive people?"

This one is powerful. It tells you a lot about how healthy their recovery *process* is and the strength of their recovery capital. A high score here often predicts improvement in all the other areas over time.

And it's a question you can work with easily:

- Who could they reconnect with?
- What positive relationship could they develop?
- What small step could strengthen their support network?

How to Improve Each Area

Here are some gentle, practical examples you can offer when someone wants to raise their score in a specific area. These are not instructions – just possibilities to explore together. The goal is always to find what feels right, safe, and manageable for them.

1. Connecting With Positive and Supportive People

If the score here is low, you might explore:

- Sending a quick message to someone they trust.
- Arranging a short check-in or coffee with a supportive friend.
- Spending time with people who make them feel calm, understood, or welcome.
- Reducing contact with people who drain their energy or add pressure.
- Asking one reliable person for a bit of practical help this week.

Small steps count – even a single positive interaction can lift the week.

2. Close Relationships

If they're struggling in this area, you might gently explore:

- Having one honest, calm conversation with a partner, family member, or friend about your struggle – and being open to their help.

- Setting a boundary to protect their energy.

- Asking for what they need rather than hoping others guess.

- Taking a small break from conflict if emotions are high.

- Let people know you appreciate their support and tell them how they can help. Sometimes patience is what you need most from those closest to you. Good communication often softens tension.

Even small shifts can improve the emotional climate.

3. Social Life and Everyday Functioning

If this score is low, think simple and doable:

- Going to one regular activity – work, class, a club, or a short shopping trip.

- Doing just the *next* thing in the day rather than

everything at once.

- Breaking tasks into tiny steps: "Put on shoes," "Go to the shop," "Buy one item."

- Attending something for ten minutes instead of the full hour.

- Asking a friend to come along if going alone feels daunting.

Recovery often shows up first in tiny bits of functioning returning – the first little break in the clouds.

4. Emotions and Feelings

When this score is low, explore:

- Taking ten minutes of quiet time each day to breathe, journal, or sit with a cup of tea.

- Talking to someone about what's weighing on them.

- Practising one small grounding technique – like noticing five things around them.

- Reducing alcohol or other substances that make

emotions even more difficult to deal with.

- Doing something soothing: a warm shower, a walk, gentle music, a favourite show, or spending a little time outdoors.

Emotional shifts don't need to be dramatic – even a small lift matters.

5. Overall Week

If this is low, explore the pattern:

- Which area pulled the week down the most?

- What's one small step that might make next week feel lighter?

- Is there one thing they could remove, reduce, or say no to?

- Is there something supportive they could add?

- Did anything go *well* this week – even something small? Celebrate that.

This question brings everything together. It helps you both see the bigger picture.

And don't forget the flip side: when scores are high or improve, ask what was different this week.

The "Overall Week" Question

This last question is simply a more general way of asking about the areas touched on in the earlier questions. In professional tools, it checks for what's called internal consistency – meaning, "Does this answer match the others?"

You don't need to worry about the technical side. Just know that it makes the overall score more sensitive to change – and that helps progress show up more clearly on the chart.

If something looks odd

If something looks off – for example, four low scores and one high – be curious. Explore it gently. There's always a story in the anomaly.

If the first question is high and the rest are low, that's actually good news: their recovery *process* is strong, even if life is heavy right now.

If only one question is low, maybe there's a single area that needs focus next week. That's useful information.

Remember the Goal: A Safe, Supportive Conversation

Above all, these questions work only when the person feels:

- Engaged
- Understood
- Safe

If they don't feel those three things, it won't help. So make safety the priority.

How to Make It Safe

- Let them know they only need to share as much as they're comfortable sharing. No pressure at all. They're already struggling – their desire to feel better is strong enough without adding any extra weight.

- Let them know that if there's a week they don't want to answer, that's completely fine.

- Let them know that if this tool doesn't feel helpful, you'll find another way together.

- Let them know there are other tools available (if you want to explore them, I cover them in my other books).

The Magic of Introducing This Questions

Most people actually like the idea of tracking their progress. It gives them hope, a sense of direction, and a clear way to talk about how they're doing. And when you reflect on their scores with them, you become an ally – and who doesn't want an ally when they're struggling?

If they're hesitant, show them how to use this tool for tracking progress with pretend answers. Let them see how the chart works. And tell them they can use it however they want:

- with you
- with someone else

- or privately, just for themselves

Giving people choice is empowering. It restores a sense of control – something distress can take away.

And honestly, simply knowing they can measure their progress often brings relief, encouragement, and a new belief that things can get better.

Step by step. Half point by half point. Week by week.

Instructions: Circle the answer that fits best for each question. Then plot your total score on the chart provided and reflect on your progress.

Not so good = 0
OK = 1
Good = 2

Week 1

Thinking about the past week...

1. **How did you do at connecting with positive and supportive people?**
   Not so good – OK – Good

2. **How were things in your close relationships?**
   Difficult – Not so good – OK

3. **How were things socially – at work, school, college, out shopping, at events, or groups you normally attend?**
   Difficult – Not so good – OK

4. **How were your emotions and feelings?**
   Difficult – Not so good – OK

5. **Overall, how was your week?**
   Difficult – Not so good – OK

Date: _____

Total score: _____

Week 2

Thinking about the past week...

1. **How did you do at connecting with positive and supportive people?**
   Not so good – OK – Good

2. **How were things in your close relationships?**
   Difficult – Not so good – OK

3. **How were things socially – at work, school, college, out shopping, at events, or groups you normally attend?**
   Difficult – Not so good – OK

4. **How were your emotions and feelings?**
   Difficult – Not so good – OK

5. **Overall, how was your week?**
   Difficult – Not so good – OK

Date: _____

Total score: _____

Week 3

Thinking about the past week...

1. **How did you do at connecting with positive and supportive people?**
   Not so good – OK – Good

2. **How were things in your close relationships?**
   Difficult – Not so good – OK

3. **How were things socially – at work, school, college, out shopping, at events, or groups you normally attend?**
   Difficult – Not so good – OK

4. **How were your emotions and feelings?**
   Difficult – Not so good – OK

5. **Overall, how was your week?**
   Difficult – Not so good – OK

Date: _____

Total score: _____

Week 4

Thinking about the past week...

1. **How did you do at connecting with positive and supportive people?**
   Not so good – OK – Good

2. **How were things in your close relationships?**
   Difficult – Not so good – OK

3. **How were things socially – at work, school, college, out shopping, at events, or groups you normally attend?**
   Difficult – Not so good – OK

4. **How were your emotions and feelings?**
   Difficult – Not so good – OK

5. **Overall, how was your week?**
   Difficult – Not so good – OK

Date: _____

Total score: _____

Week 5

Thinking about the past week...

1. **How did you do at connecting with positive and supportive people?**
   Not so good – OK – Good

2. **How were things in your close relationships?**
   Difficult – Not so good – OK

3. **How were things socially – at work, school, college, out shopping, at events, or groups you normally attend?**
   Difficult – Not so good – OK

4. **How were your emotions and feelings?**
   Difficult – Not so good – OK

5. **Overall, how was your week?**
   Difficult – Not so good – OK

Date: _____

Total score: _____

Week 6

Thinking about the past week...

1. **How did you do at connecting with positive and supportive people?**
Not so good – OK – Good

2. **How were things in your close relationships?**
Difficult – Not so good – OK

3. **How were things socially – at work, school, college, out shopping, at events, or groups you normally attend?**
Difficult – Not so good – OK

4. **How were your emotions and feelings?**
Difficult – Not so good – OK

5. **Overall, how was your week?**
Difficult – Not so good – OK

Date: _____

Total score: _____

Week 7

Thinking about the past week...

1. **How did you do at connecting with positive and supportive people?**
   Not so good – OK – Good

2. **How were things in your close relationships?**
   Difficult – Not so good – OK

3. **How were things socially – at work, school, college, out shopping, at events, or groups you normally attend?**
   Difficult – Not so good – OK

4. **How were your emotions and feelings?**
   Difficult – Not so good – OK

5. **Overall, how was your week?**
   Difficult – Not so good – OK

Date: _____

Total score: _____

Week 8

Thinking about the past week...

1. **How did you do at connecting with positive and supportive people?**
   Not so good – OK – Good

2. **How were things in your close relationships?**
   Difficult – Not so good – OK

3. **How were things socially – at work, school, college, out shopping, at events, or groups you normally attend?**
   Difficult – Not so good – OK

4. **How were your emotions and feelings?**
   Difficult – Not so good – OK

5. **Overall, how was your week?**
   Difficult – Not so good – OK

Date: _____

Total score: _____

HELP A FRIEND RECOVER

Score

10	o	o	o	o	o	o	o	o
9	o	o	o	o	o	o	o	o
8	o	o	o	o	o	o	o	o
7	o	o	o	o	o	o	o	o
6	o	o	o	o	o	o	o	o
5	o	o	o	o	o	o	o	o
4	o	o	o	o	o	o	o	o
3	o	o	o	o	o	o	o	o
2	o	o	o	o	o	o	o	o
1	o	o	o	o	o	o	o	o
0	o	o	o	o	o	o	o	o
Week →	1	2	3	4	5	6	7	8

Each week, mark the circle that matches your total score.

Consider the follow as guidelines for interpreting your score:

- 8–10: Doing OK – still worth talking through the week.

- 5–7: Concerning – something is affecting your wellbeing.

- 0–4: Very concerning – you are likely really struggling and should consider seek support.

Chapter Four

Help Them Learn New Skills

Look over these skill sheets with the person you're supporting and ask which skills they'd like to learn or strengthen. Give them time. Let them browse, think, and notice what feels most useful or hopeful to them right now.

Then, together, choose two or three skills from the sheet they're most interested in. Focus on these for the coming week. Keep it simple and manageable – small steps work best. Think about the situations where they can practise each skill and what that might look like in real life. The aim isn't to master everything at once, but to build confidence, one skill at a time.

Return to this process each week. Review what they practised, celebrate any progress, and learn from the weeks when progress wasn't made – knowing what doesn't work is also part of the skill-building process. Then choose the next skill to explore. Over time, these small, consistent choices create momentum. You'll be amazed at how quickly someone can grow when they feel supported, guided, and encouraged to try something new.

Skillset 1: Managing and Reducing Cravings

1. **Practice distraction**
   Go for a walk. Talk to a friend about sport. Draw a picture – even if you can't draw very well. Read a joke book. Try things out and discover what helps you manage and reduce your cravings.

2. **Have a chat with someone who understands**
   Talk with a counsellor or another person in recovery about your cravings.

3. **Stay motivated**
   Remind yourself why you've stopped using or cut down. Write a list. Keep a picture or note in your pocket that reminds you why you're doing this and look at it when you feel tempted. Review your reasons for stopping with a friend or Recovery Peer. Calculate the savings and benefits of stopping or reducing.

4. **Stay busy**
   Plan your day. Don't leave too much spare time or space for boredom if these are triggers.

5. **Breathe**

    Take some deep, slow breaths. Try taking 10 slow breaths in a row and then see how you feel. If the cravings are still there, try another 10 until they ease.

6. **Try something new**

    Some people find yoga, acupuncture, or meditation helpful.

7. **Do a good deed**

    Focus on helping others – it gives the cravings less room to take over.

8. **Don't give up**

    Recovery has ups and downs, good days and difficult days. Keep moving forward, even if there are occasional setbacks.

9. **Visualise**

    Picture a pleasant image in your mind – a place you've been or somewhere you'd love to go. Imagine what it feels like to be there: the smells, sights, and textures. Is it warm or cold? Is there a breeze?

10. **Cravings are normal**

    Recognise that cravings are normal. Don't feel bad about them. Feel good – you're making a positive decision and taking charge of your life. Cravings lessen over time as you grow stronger in your recovery and fill your life with positive people, places, and experiences.

11. **Try accepting your cravings**

    Accept them. Don't fight them. Allow yourself to experience them and let them pass naturally.

12. **Fast forward**

    Think ahead to what will happen if you use. Consider the negative consequences and the positive things that will come if you resist.

13. **Surf the urge**

    Imagine cravings as a wave you can ride until it passes.

14. **Get rid of things that trigger you**

    Remove items in your living space that trigger cravings.

15. **Avoid temptation**
    Avoid the people, places, and activities that tempt you to use. Replace them with positive people, places, and patterns.

16. **Avoid getting too hungry, tired, angry, or lonely**
    Focus on good self-care. Make a plan to look after yourself each day and discuss it with a friend or Recovery Peer.

17. **Your cravings will pass**
    Remind yourself that cravings always pass – they usually ease after about 10 minutes or so.

18. **Make Nice Cup of Tea**

    Slowly go through the process of making a cup of tea – at half, or even a quarter, pace.

    Notice each sense as you go.

    Turn the tap on. Let the water run through your fingers for a moment, feel of the water as it pours into the kettle, notice the vibration and sound as it begins to boil, experience the splash of the hot water hitting the mug.

Take in the smell as the tea steeps, watch the milk swirl, feel the warmth of the mug in your hands.

As you take a sip, notice the taste and temperature. Pause for a moment.

Feel the weight of the mug, and listen to the sound it makes as you place it back down.

And, as if by magic, your cravings may just have disappeared.

Skillset 2: Healthy Stress Coping Skills

1. **Listen to your wise mind**
   Find a quiet place and time to connect with your inner wisdom – the answers are often already there.

2. **List your options**
   In every situation, you have choices. Write them down if it helps.

3. **Choose self-respect**
   Choose the option that will help you like yourself tomorrow.

4. **Compassion**
   Treat yourself with respect, acceptance, and gentleness.

5. **Use compassionate self-talk**
   Speak to yourself with the same kindness you'd offer a friend.

6. **Use your imagination**
   Think of things, images, or memories that help

you feel calmer or safer.

7. **Be creative**
Write, paint, sculpt, sing, dance – expression helps release tension.

8. **Distract yourself**
Watch a funny show, read a book, admire a sunset, listen to calming music.

9. **Be nice to yourself**
In difficult times, take care of yourself: enjoy a warm bath, do some yoga, connect with a friend.

10. **Spend time with animals or in nature**
Both can soothe the mind and reduce stress.

11. **Remind yourself that it will pass**
Difficult feelings fade with time; they never stay forever.

12. **Take good care of yourself**
Eat well, sleep enough, move your body, practise safe sex – self-care strengthens resilience.

13. **Do the best you can with what you have**

Work with the options available to you, even if they're small.

14. Find meaning
Remind yourself of what matters to you and what you're living for.

15. Ask for help
Reach out to someone safe and supportive.

16. Inspire yourself
Carry something positive – a poem, quote, or picture – to remind you of hope.

17. Remember the past
Recall how far you've already come; let that motivate you to keep going.

18. Leave a bad scene
If things escalate or feel unsafe, step away.

19. Be persistent
Never, never, never give up. Keep moving forward, even in tiny steps.

20. Honesty

Secrets and lies often sit at the heart of problems. Be honest with someone safe. Honesty heals.

21. **Cry**

Let yourself cry. Tears help release pressure and emotion.

22. **Set a boundary**

Protect yourself by saying "no" when you need to.

Skillset 3: Healthy Sleeping Habits

1. **Go to bed and wake up at regular times**
   Keeping consistent sleep and wake times helps regulate your body clock.

2. **Create a bedtime routine to wind down**
   A calming routine signals to your body that it's time to sleep.

3. **Develop a regular daytime schedule**
   Having structure during the day supports better sleep at night.

4. **Improve your sleep environment**
   Make your bedroom comfortable, quiet, dark, and cool to promote rest.

5. **Get out of bed if you can't sleep**
   If you're still awake after about 30 minutes, get up and do something relaxing until you feel sleepy again.

6. **Exercise regularly during the day**
   Physical activity helps sleep – just avoid intense

exercise close to bedtime.

7. **Reduce tea and coffee**
Cut down on caffeine during the day, especially in the afternoon and evening.

8. **Don't worry about not sleeping**
Worry makes sleep harder. Remind yourself that sleep will come in time.

9. **Avoid stimulants before bed**
Stay away from sugary foods, smoking, and caffeine in the hours before bedtime.

10. **Avoid daytime naps**
If you do nap, keep it short and at the same time each day.

Skillset 4: Managing Anger in a Healthy Way

1. **Become aware of what contributes to your anger**
   Notice the situations, thoughts, and pressures that lead to anger – uncertainty, relationship stress, overthinking, money worries, or certain environments.

2. **Become aware of what contributes to your calmness**
   Identify the things that help you stay steady – self-confidence, supportive friends, planning ahead, or hobbies you enjoy.

3. **Learn what helps you control your temper**
   Explore the actions that calm you: walking away, avoiding conflict, talking with a friend, crying, counting to ten, taking deep breaths, exercising, using positive self-talk, spending time with calming people, or using the Temper Thermometer.

4. **Use the Temper Thermometer**
   Your Recovery Peer will explain how it works and

how it can help you track rising tension.

5. **Channel your anger into assertiveness, not aggression**
An assertiveness plan helps you set clear, reasonable goals and work toward them without harming or offending anyone. It may take longer, but it prevents far more problems.

6. **Become aware of your expectations**
Develop reasonable expectations of others. Unrealistic expectations often fuel anger.

7. **Talk things through with someone you trust**
Share what's going on in a way that helps you feel calmer afterwards.

8. **Pause for a minute.**
Take a breath, and look at your options.

You can:
Work it out.
Wait it out.
Walk it out.
Talk it out.

GEARÓID CAREY

Figure it out.
Write it out.

Just don't act it out.

Skillset 5: Relationship Skills

1. **Become more aware of the qualities of healthy relationships**
   These include being trusting, respectful, supportive, accepting, understanding, and encouraging.

2. **Become more aware of the qualities of unhealthy relationships**
   These include criticising, threatening, punishing, complaining, controlling, and blaming.

3. **Reflect on past supportive relationships**
   List and talk about some of the healthy, encouraging relationships you've had in the past.

4. **Identify healthy relationships in your life now**
   Talk about the people who currently bring support, positivity, and stability into your life.

5. **Make a plan to spend more time with positive people**
   Choose to be around those who uplift and en-

courage you.

6. **Make a plan to spend more time in positive places**
Go to places where you're likely to meet supportive people – the library, the gym, support groups, work, education settings, or faith-based activities.

Skillset 6: Grounding Skills

Practical things people can do to reduce mental-health symptoms in the moment.

1. **Name five things you can see**
   Look around and say them out loud – colours, shapes, objects. This anchors your mind to the room you're in.

2. **Feel your feet on the floor**
   Notice the pressure, the temperature, the weight of your body being supported.

3. **Take slow, steady breaths**
   In for four seconds, out for six. Repeat until your body settles.

4. **Hold something with texture**
   A stone, a piece of fabric, a cold can, a stress ball – focus on how it feels.

5. **Run cold water over your hands**
   Cold sensation brings you back into your body quickly.

6. **Notice 5–4–3–2–1**

    - 5 things you can see
    - 4 things you can feel
    - 3 things you can hear
    - 2 things you can smell
    - 1 thing you can taste

7. **Say the date, time, and your name out loud**
   This reminds your mind that you're safe right now.

8. **Count backwards slowly from 100**
   If you lose your place, start again – it focuses and steadies the mind.

9. **Move your body gently**
   Stretch, roll your shoulders, walk to another room, or shake out your hands.

10. **Look for something in the room of a specific colour**
    "All the blue things" – simple, but it redirects the

brain.

11. Hum or sing a familiar tune
Vibration helps regulate the nervous system.

12. Ground through temperature
Hold an ice cube, sip a warm drink, or use a cool cloth on your face.

13. Describe your surroundings in detail
Say aloud: "I am in my bedroom. The walls are white. The lamp is on…"
Keep describing until your body begins to settle.

14. Touch something comforting
A blanket, a jumper, a scented hand cream – soothing textures help bring you back.

15. Use your senses intentionally
Light a candle, smell essential oils, taste a mint – one strong sense can cut through overwhelm.

16. Press your hands together firmly
Notice the muscles engaging. Slow, deliberate pressure helps anchor you.

17. **Remind yourself where you are and that you're safe**

    A simple phrase like: *"This feeling will pass. I'm safe. I can handle this."*

18. **Do a quick mental task**

    Spell your name backwards, list the months of the year, or name all the cities you can think of. Cognitive tasks interrupt spirals.

19. **Step outside for fresh air**

    Feel the temperature, hear the sounds, breathe slowly.

20. **Ground through movement**

    Walk slowly and pay attention to each step – heel, foot, toes.

21. **Splash your face with water**

    The sudden change in temperature helps reset your nervous system

22. **Put your hands in earth**

    Soil, sand, or grass – natural textures can be deeply grounding.

23. **Spend time with animals**

    Petting, holding, or simply sitting with an animal can calm the body and mind.

Skillset 7: Practical Ways to Deal with Depression

Here's a list of ideas that can help you cope and, in time, move forward. Use the ones that feel right for you.

You don't have to read through them all at once – just look at a few each day.

And as you do, remember that each one has the potential to become a small building block in your recovery.

1. **Have reasonable expectations of yourself.**
   Stop expecting your "normal" output. When you're struggling, everyday tasks take more energy. It's OK to ask less of yourself – and to be pleased when you get those things done.

2. **Anchor the day with one fixed point.**
   A regular action, done at the same time and in the same place, helps create predictability and relax the nervous system. This could be as simple as a morning drink, a brief walk, or sitting quietly in the same spot each day.

3. **Move your body gently.**
   Try brief walks or light stretching. Done consistently, gentle movement gives the body regular opportunities to reset and regain a little energy each time. In time, making this a simple daily routine – same time, same place, same gentle movement – can help reduce symptoms and slowly build momentum for healing.

4. **Get daylight.**
   Get outdoors into natural light. Even a few minutes, a few times a day, can help. Daylight plays an important role in regulating sleep and mood cycles.

5. **Eat something regularly.**
   Skipping meals can worsen mood instability and leave you feeling more irritable or flat. Regular eating helps steady energy and mood, even if meals are simple and small. Perfection isn't required – eating something is better than eating nothing. Even when you don't feel like eating, having a small, nutritious snack at regular times during the day can help.

6. **Hydrate before you interpret how you feel.**
Poor hydration can contribute to emotional flatness or agitation. Make drinking water a routine part of your day. Maybe add some lemon juice or get some sparkling wate can make it more interesting.

7. **Reduce decision load.**
For example, prepare your clothes the night before and keep things simple. Try not to fill your day with important choices. When you're experiencing depression, you have a limited daily budget for decision-making – protect it.

8. **Eat simply.**
Eat simple, nutritious meals that don't require much effort – scrambled eggs, two well-peppered pork chops, or a quick salad with grated cheese. Simplifying choices and eating the same meals at the same time can be helpful; for example, having bacon and eggs most mornings. Many people find diet an important factor in stabilising mood, so notice how you feel after different meals and see what works for you. Keeping things simple makes

it easier to get the nourishment you need without feeling overwhelmed by options.

9. **Name what's happening.**
Saying "this is depression" can reduce – or even avoid – self-blame and confusion. When you name the experience, it helps separate what's happening from who you are. Instead of seeing difficulties as personal failure, you can recognise them as part of a temporary state that needs care and support.

10. **Practise compassionate self-talk.**
Notice how you speak to yourself when things feel hard. Depression often comes with harsh self-criticism, which increases distress rather than helping. Being hard on yourself over even small things is, in fact, a common feature of depression. Responding with compassion – as you would to someone you care about – can reduce emotional strain and make it easier to keep going. You might say things like: *"I am doing the best I can at the moment,"* or *"Right now, I need to focus on self-care, and in time I'll be stronger."*

11. **Track mood or distress briefly.**

    Using a simple 0–10 scale once a day can build awareness and restore a sense of movement. Even when things feel stuck, tracking helps you notice small changes over time and reminds you that how you feel doesn't stay constant – change is often happening if you take the time to notice it.

    Let 0 mean "as bad as it can get" and 10 mean feeling good, with no significant symptoms of depression. You might check in a few times a day by asking yourself, *"Where am I from 0 to 10?"* If you're doing well, ask yourself, *"What's helping right now, and how can I sustain this?"* If your score is low, focus on small, manageable acts of self-care rather than trying to fix everything – this is often an effective way to avoid berating yourself.

12. **Break tasks down to the first physical step.**

    Instead of "clean the house," focus on something concrete like "stand up" or "tidy one item or one small area." Depression often makes planning and motivation harder, so reducing tasks to the very first physical action lowers the barrier to starting. Once movement begins, the next step often becomes easier to see. When you're ready, you can then take on the next practical step.

13. **Reach out for emotional support in small steps.**
You don't have to explain everything at once. Small connections matter – a short text saying "Hi," or a message to a friend like "Can we catch up? It would be good to talk," if that feels right. You might then start with a brief phone conversation, opening up just a little. You may be surprised how, when people know you need support, they often care deeply and want to help. Try to make reaching out to your supports a regular habit, even when it doesn't feel easy. Sometimes simply sitting with someone and having a cuppa can make a difference – no deep conversation required, just the comfort of knowing you're not alone.

14. **Limit rumination windows.**
Rumination that leaves you feeling worse can feel hard to break free from during periods of de-

pression, but giving it a clear boundary can help. Allow yourself a short, defined window – such as 10 minutes – to think things through, then gently shift your attention elsewhere.

If you notice yourself dwelling on the same thoughts again later, you can give it another brief 10-minute window, then move on by redirecting your attention. Simple distractions or grounding activities can help – for example, doing a small task or splashing cold water on your face before shifting to a new, healthier focus. This approach helps stop rumination from taking over the day while still acknowledging that something is on your mind.

Over time, this practice can start to happen more automatically as self-awareness and mindfulness grow.

15. **Connect with professional support.**
Staying connected with professional support can make a real difference, especially when things feel overwhelming. Making and keeping appoint-

ments can be challenging during depression, but regular contact helps maintain continuity and perspective while gradually building momentum. Even when it's hard, staying connected helps ensure you're not facing things alone and provides ongoing support as recovery unfolds.

16. **Develop structure first, then motivation.**
When depression is present, waiting to feel motivated can keep you stuck. Simple structure – such as a set time to get up, eat, or step outside – can help you take action even when motivation is low. For example, you might make a habit of taking a short walk each morning, regardless of how you feel. Saying a brief prayer or meditation before bed each night can also provide a steady routine. Often, motivation follows once you begin, rather than needing to come first.

17. **Create a "minimum viable day."**
Decide in advance what counts as "enough" for today, and allow yourself to stop there. On difficult days, setting a low, realistic threshold – such as getting up, eating something, and leaving the

house briefly – can prevent burnout and reduce self-criticism. Anything beyond that is a bonus, not a requirement.

If a whole day feels like too much, break it down further. You might create a simple "minimum viable" plan for the morning, then one for the afternoon, and another for the evening. When needed, reduce it again – just plan for the next hour, or even the next 15 minutes.

18. **Limit alcohol and depressant substances.**
Many people find it helpful to reduce or avoid alcohol and other substances during periods of depression. Doing so can support recovery and help you progress more quickly. It's something worth considering – you might try it out for a day or two and notice how it affects your mood and progress overall.

19. **Sleep at roughly the same time.**
Going to bed and getting up at similar times each day helps regulate your body clock, which can support mood and energy. Regular sleep matters

more than perfect sleep – consistency helps even when sleep itself isn't great.

If you wake up and can't get back to sleep, try not to lie there getting frustrated. After a few minutes, get up briefly and do something gentle – stretch, take a sip of water, or rest your mind with a short prayer or meditation – then lie down again.

20. **Engage your senses.**
Depression can dull sensation and pull your attention into a narrow, negative way of thinking. Deliberately engaging the senses helps bring you back into the present moment and can gently lift emotional flatness. Simple activities – such as a warm shower, listening to music, tasting strong flavours, noticing a comforting scent, or holding textured objects – can ground you in your body and provide brief relief from mental heaviness.

21. **Do something mildly absorbing.**
Activities that gently hold your attention can give your mind a break from repetitive thinking with-

out demanding too much energy. Simple tasks – such as puzzles, building something, organising a small space, or colouring in – can create a sense of calm focus.

22. **Limit exposure to draining media.**
News cycles and social media feeds can quietly worsen mood, increase anxiety, and pull attention toward negative or overwhelming content. Reducing exposure – or placing limits on what you watch – even temporarily, can help protect emotional energy and make space for recovery. This might mean setting time limits, avoiding certain topics for a while, or choosing calmer, more nourishing content instead.

23. **Ask for practical help.**
When you're feeling low, explaining how you feel can be exhausting or overwhelming. Asking for practical help – "Can you help me with X?" – is often easier and more effective in the moment. Small, concrete support can reduce load, build connection, and make things feel more manageable without needing a deep emotional conversa-

tion.

24. **Re-establish one social role.**

    Depression often disrupts our sense of purpose and belonging. Reconnecting with just one role – such as parent, worker, friend, or volunteer – even in a reduced or limited way, can help restore structure and meaning. This might mean being present for part of the day as a parent, sending one message as a friend, or doing a small task at work or in the community. You don't need to do everything you once did; simply showing up in a small, manageable way can remind you that you still have a place and a contribution.

25. **Notice small improvements.**

    Depression rarely lifts all at once; it usually loosens in small increments. Paying attention to small improvements – feeling a little better on a brief walk, enjoying a conversation with a friend, or having a better night's sleep – can guide you toward what's working and provide encouragement to keep going.

Small improvements matter, and noticing them helps you build recovery step by step rather than waiting for a sudden shift.

26. **Stop arguing with your thoughts.**
When you're depressed, thoughts can become repetitive, harsh, or unhelpful. Trying to argue with them or prove them wrong often keeps you stuck in mental loops. You don't need to win debates with your mind to recover – noticing thoughts, letting them pass, and gently returning your attention to what you're doing is often more effective.

27. **Seek support that focuses on outcomes.**
Understanding why you feel the way you do can be helpful, but what ultimately matters is what reduces distress and improves daily functioning. Support that regularly checks whether things are actually getting better – and adjusts when they're not – tends to be more effective than insight alone.

Recovery is less about having the perfect explanation and more about noticing real-world change and what helps you progress.

28. **Allow time to do its work.**
Healing has its own pace. With time, small efforts add up, and change begins to grow in its own quiet way.

All of these small things add up, and slowly recovery begins to take hold – even if it doesn't feel that way on some days.

And as you measure your progress each week, you'll soon learn what works for you.

Skillset 8: Practical Ways for Dealing With Anxiety

Here's a list of practical things you can do to reduce anxiety in the moment.

Use the ones that feel right for you.

1. **Slow the exhale.**
   Breathe in for a comfortable count, then breathe out for a slightly longer count. Extending the out-breath helps reduce physiological arousal and allows the body to settle by emptying the lungs more fully and encouraging deeper breathing. Even two or three of these breaths can take the edge off anxiety, and a minute or two can make a noticeable difference.

2. **Put your feet flat on the floor.**
   While sitting, place both feet firmly on the ground and notice the sensation. This kind of physical grounding can quickly steady the body when anxiety rises.

3. **Name five things you can see.**

Slowly look around and name five things in your environment. This helps shift attention out of anxious thinking and into the present moment.

Alternatively, pick one object and notice five things about it – its colour, texture, shape, weight, and temperature.

4. **Relax your shoulders.**
Drop your shoulders and gently move them in small circles. Releasing tension here can help the body settle when anxiety rises.

5. **Change your posture.**
Gently shift into a more upright posture. Lengthen your spine, let your shoulders move back slightly, and lift your chin just enough to align your neck. This kind of posture can promote a sense of confidence – signalling to your body that you can deal with what's happening.

6. **Splash cold water on your face.**
Or hold something cold, like an ice cube or a chilled bottle. Sudden cold stimulation can interrupt rising panic and refocus your attention,

often providing quick relief when anxiety feels intense. It can act like a wake-up call, bringing you back to the here and now.

7. **Breathe in through your nose and out through your mouth.**

    Breathing in and out through your mouth can subtly signal alarm to the body and keep it in a more alert, stress-ready state, as it indicates a need for increased oxygen in preparation for fight or flight. Breathing in through the nose and out through the mouth signals safety to the nervous system and supports calmer, steadier thinking. If you notice yourself breathing through your mouth, gently switch your breathing pattern. Even a short period of breathing this way can help reduce anxious intensity.

8. **Slow your movements.**

    Deliberately move more slowly for a few minutes – even at half or quarter speed. This might be while walking, or even while sipping a glass of water. You may be surprised how this affects your thoughts, feelings, perceptions, and body.

9. **Press your palms together tightly, then relax.**
   Brief muscle tension followed by release helps ground the body. The contrast between tension and rest can help the nervous system reset and settle.

   What matters most is noticing how this affects you. Practising mindfulness as you do it – paying attention to shifts in your body, focus, and feelings – helps you recognise the difference it makes.

10. **Look around and orient.**
    Take a moment to quietly name where you are and what day it is. Orienting yourself like this helps anchor you in the present and reminds you that you are here, now, and safe. It can be especially helpful when anxiety makes things feel unreal, overwhelming, or out of control.

11. **Focus your self-talk.**
    Say things to yourself – out loud if you can – that help reduce anxiety and steady you in the moment. Simple phrases like "I am safe," "I have the skills I need to manage this," or "This moment

will pass; I just need to breathe through it" can be grounding as anxiety rises.

Find phrases or short mantras that guide and support you through moments of intense or severe anxiety.

12. **Practise a half smile.**
Gently lifting the corners of your mouth into a small, relaxed smile can subtly affect your feelings and physiology. Try it now and notice whether you feel a slight change when you do.

13. **Hum softly**
Gentle humming can relax the mind and body a little. Humming is one of the simplest ways to soothe your nervous system – no skill, privacy, or preparation required.

A few subtle things are happening when you hum:
– It naturally slows your breathing.
– Humming lengthens the exhale, which tells the body that it's safe to relax.

– The vibration has a grounding effect.
– Feeling the sound in your chest or lips draws attention away from your thoughts.

The mind can't hum and race at the same time. Even a soft, steady tone can interrupt anxious or looping thoughts. It's emotionally regulating.

Many people instinctively hum when comforting a baby. That same soothing mechanism works for adults too.

There's no right note, tune, or volume. You can hum while sitting, walking, or lying down. A few breaths worth is often enough to take the edge off.

14. **Play a musical instrument.**

You dont have to be good at it. Truly. Just play.

Playing an instrument isn't about performance, talent, or getting it right. It's about entering a different mental state—one where attention narrows, the inner critic quiets, and your nervous system settles.

When you play, even clumsily, a few important things happen:
Your mind slows down.
– Music pulls attention into the present moment. Thoughts that were looping or racing tend to loosen their grip because your focus is gently occupied.
– Emotion gets a safe outlet.
– Music allows feeling to move without needing words. You can express tension, sadness, restlessness, or joy without analysing any of it.
– The body and mind sync up.
– Rhythm, breath, and movement begin to align. This has a naturally regulating effect on stress and anxiety.

There's no pressure to succeed. Unlike many things in life, playing an instrument can exist without goals, outcomes, or judgment. You're allowed to be messy, repetitive, and imperfect. Just let it flow.

This could be a guitar, piano, keyboard, drum,

violin, or even a simple instrument you've never played before. Five minutes is enough. Ten is plenty. There's no need to practise scales or learn songs unless you want to.

15. **Sigh.**
    This really can make a difference – try it and notice for yourself.

16. **Limit input.**
    Reducing noise, screens, or visual clutter helps you return to a calmer state.

17. **Slow your speech.**
    Speaking a little more slowly, with pauses or even gentle breaths between sentences, often reduces anxiety.

    Anxiety often speeds up language – both out loud and internally. Deliberately slowing your speech, including your inner voice, sends a signal to the mind and body that there's no immediate threat, reducing the sense of urgency and danger.

18. **Put one hand on your chest.**

Placing a hand on your chest can feel comforting and grounding, helping ease anxious intensity in the moment.

19. **Connect with people you feel safe with.**
Give them a call, send a text, or invite them over for a coffee. Even small contact – getting a message back or knowing someone is coming round – can reduce feelings of isolation and anxiety.

20. **Ask yourself one practical question**
When your mind feels overloaded or stuck, bring it back to ground level by asking: *"What's the next small thing I need to do?"*

This gently shifts you out of worry and into action. You're not trying to solve everything – just identifying the very next step. Even a tiny, practical action can restore a sense of control and momentum, and once that step is done, the next one often becomes clearer on its own.

21. **This experience is not permanent**
Gently remind yourself: *"This is anxiety. It will rise and fall – and on some days, it will fade away."*

Anxiety often feels endless when you're in it, but it's a temporary state, not a fixed condition. Naming it for what it is creates a little distance, and remembering that it naturally peaks and subsides can reduce the fear that something is wrong – or that it will never pass.

22. **Drop the struggle – accept it**
Let the feeling be there without trying to push it away. Resisting anxiety often makes it louder and more persistent, while allowing it – without judgment – takes away much of its power. Acceptance isn't giving up; it's recognising that you can tolerate the feeling as it passes through on its own.

23. **Reduce urgency**
Remind yourself: *"Nothing needs to be decided right now."*

Anxiety creates a false sense of emergency, pushing you to think and act before you're ready. Slowing things down helps your nervous system settle and allows clearer thinking to return. Most decisions improve when given time – and very few truly need to be made in this moment.

24. **Engage one sense fully**

    Choose a single sense – taste, smell, or sound – and give it your full attention. This gently anchors you in the present moment and draws your mind away from anxious thinking. Even a few seconds of focused sensory awareness can help your body settle and restore a sense of steadiness. It often helps to focus on pleasant sensations.

25. **Step outside briefly**

    A simple change of environment can help reset your system. Fresh air, natural light, or just a few moments away from where you were can interrupt anxious momentum and give your mind and body a chance to settle.

    Step outside, take a deep breath, swing your arms a little, and give it a few minutes – then notice how you feel.

26. **Don't feed it**

    Anxiety peaks and passes if it's not fed. By staying

with the feeling – without reacting, analysing, or trying to escape – you allow it to run its course. Each time you do this, you strengthen the knowledge that you can tolerate the sensation and that it will pass on its own. *Wait it out, deliberately.*

Often, it's a combination of these that helps reduce anxiety in the moment – and makes the day easier to manage.

Keep this list handy, and when your anxiety rises, look through it and pick one or two things to try.

Skillset 9: Helpful Tips If You Hear Voices

Practical things people can do to reduce distress in the moment and, over time, lessen the frequency and intensity of voices.

1. **Ground yourself in the present**
   Name where you are, what day it is, and what you're doing right now.

2. **Shift attention to the body**
   Notice your feet on the floor, your back against the chair, your breath moving in and out.

3. **Lower arousal first**
   Slowing your breathing or relaxing muscles often reduces how intrusive voices feel.

4. **Respond, don't react**
   Pausing before engaging with voices gives you back a small but important choice.

5. **Limit arguing with voices**
   Direct confrontation often increases intensity for many people.

6. **Use brief, firm boundaries**
Short phrases like "Not now" or "I'm busy" are often more effective than debate.

7. **Engage in a focusing activity**
Reading aloud, puzzles, music, or organising can pull attention elsewhere.

8. **Use sound deliberately**
Background noise, headphones, or music can reduce the clarity and dominance of voices.

9. **Ground through movement**
Walking, stretching, or light physical tasks can interrupt escalation.

10. **Notice patterns over time**
Track when voices are louder – stress, fatigue, and isolation often play a role.

11. **Reduce overall stress load where possible**
Fewer demands often means fewer or quieter voices.

12. **Prioritise consistent sleep**
Irregular or poor sleep commonly increases in-

tensity.

13. Eat regularly
A poor diet can worsen distress and perceptual experiences.

14. Limit alcohol and stimulants
These often amplify voices, even if they feel calming in the short term.

15. Anchor attention externally
Describe objects around you in detail to stay oriented outward.

16. Use compassionate self-talk
Reassuring yourself can reduce fear, which often feeds voices.

17. Avoid fighting for total control
Aiming for less distress is often more effective than trying to silence voices.

18. Create a personal coping plan
Decide in advance what helps when voices intensify. Do some research and see what works for others.

19. **Write down what the voices say – then set it aside**
Externalising can reduce their hold without engaging with the content.

20. **Increase safe social contact**
Being around others often reduces intrusiveness, even without conversation.

21. **Reclaim meaningful roles**
Purpose and structure can weaken the grip of voices over time.

22. **Develop a strong sense of self and your values**
Remind yourself of what matters most to you. This can reduce the influence of the voices.

23. **Focus on the task at hand**
Bring your attention to what you're doing right now – making the bed, eating breakfast, or going for a brisk walk.

24. **Choose a task**
Pick a task you know works for you, such as gardening or brushing your pets.

25. **Distract yourself**
    Do whatever helps in that moment – watch a short, funny video, listen to your favourite song, or whistle a tune.

26. **Notice when voices soften**
    Paying attention to improvement – however small – matters. Notice what's different: your surroundings, your focus, or how your day has been.

27. **Seek support focused on coping, not labels**
    Practical help and coping strategies often matter more than explanations.

28. **Give change time**
    Reduced distress usually comes first; frequency and intensity often follow later.

In time, you'll discover what works best for you. These ideas are just a starting point – try the ones that make sense to you and adapt them over time.

The voices often lessen, and may even fade with time. But even before that, you can learn to manage them well enough that they no longer cause fear or distress or influence your choices. From there, you can work toward your goals, be more present in the moment, and live the life you want to live.

Skillset 10: Helpful Tips If You Experience an Unshared Reality

Sometimes, we believe things that no one else seems to believe. These experiences can be thought of as unshared realities. They feel completely real to the person experiencing them, even if others don't share them.

Here are some ways to work with these experiences so they interfere less with daily life – and so that, over time, they may become clearer, more manageable, and more open to re-evaluation.

You may hear these experiences referred to as delusions. If that word doesn't sit well with you, that's okay. What matters most is finding a way of understanding what's happening that helps you cope and regain steadiness.

Even years after my last mental-health episode, I sometimes wake in the night caught inside an unshared reality – truly believing terrible things are happening and that there's no way to escape them. Over time, I've learned not to fight the experience in the moment. I wait until the sun rises. By then, the experience has faded enough for me to look at it from a distance – and recognise it for what it was.

Everyone finds their own way of managing these experiences. There's no single right approach. What follows are some ideas that may help you live with an unshared reality more safely and with less disruption to your life.

And while others may not share your experience, wise and compassionate people can still understand this: the experience is real for you at that moment. When others can hold that understanding, they can help you manage the experience without dismissing or invalidating it.

1. **Pause when everything feels urgent**
   If life suddenly feels like you're inside a terrifying, high-stakes film, pause. Delaying action – even briefly – gives you time to regain perspective, and often clarity.

2. **Slow things down**
   When others don't share your experience, slow down.

3. *Relabel the experience*
   If everyone else seems to believe what you're experiencing isn't real, take a breath and step back. Slowly and calmly say to yourself, "This may be a

delusion." This can weaken its pull and give you time to process the experience more slowly.

4. **Focus on impact, not truth.**
   Ask: "Is engaging with this helping or harming me or others right now?"

   If it can wait, let it wait.

   If it can't wait, ask:
   "What is the least I need to do right now to address my thoughts and experience?"
   "What response carries the least risk or potential harm?"

5. **Lower arousal first**
   High stress strengthens certainty. Calm the body before evaluating beliefs.

6. **Ground in shared reality**
   Anchor attention to time, place, and the observations you do share with others.

7. **Use written reality-checking**
   Write the belief down and revisit it later, rather

than engaging immediately.

8. **Delay decisions linked to the belief**
Important choices can wait until you're feeling calmer.

9. **Reduce isolation**
Being around others often softens conviction, even without discussion.

10. **Notice emotional fuel**
Fear, anger, or excitement often intensify unshared realities. Do some grounding exercises and see how they are then.

11. **Shift attention deliberately**
Engage in neutral, absorbing activities to reduce mental grip.

12. **Use probability language**
Replace certainty ("this is happening") with possibility ("this might be").

13. **Ask a stabilising question**
"What's the safest response right now?"

14. **Maintain daily routines**

    Structure supports stability and helps reconnect with a more grounded reality over time.

15. **Protect sleep**

    Sleep disruption and deprivation can be a major amplifier of unshared realities.

16. **Limit substances**

    Alcohol and stimulants commonly increase certainty and intensity.

17. **Identify personal warning signs**

    Notice early cues that clarity may be slipping, and have plans in place for these moments that help you stay grounded and avoid escalation.

18. **Create a personal coping plan**

    Decide in advance what helps when beliefs begin to strengthen.

19. **Develop allies**

    Share these plans with trusted people in your life so they know how to support you when beliefs intensify. This helps those who care about you know how to help you best.

20. **Use trusted reality anchors**
    A person, place, or activity that reliably grounds you.

21. **Avoid arguing with yourself**
    Heated internal debates often entrench beliefs rather than loosen them

    Calm, slowed-down reasoning is more likely to allow a new perspective to emerge. Even a small shift can be helpful – for example, moving from "This is really happening" to "This feels so real."

22. **Practice "holding lightly"**
    These thoughts and beliefs don't have to dominate what you're doing right now. You also don't have to decide whether they're true right now. You have choices. Remind yourself that you have choices in how you respond to this experience. You might write down different options for dealing with these thoughts and feelings, then consider which response is safest and wisest.

23. **Reinforce the observing self**

    The part of you that can question is a strength – cultivate it. Practice stepping back and observing your thoughts and experiences from a little distance. You may notice something that helps you respond more wisely.

24. **Step outside of yourself**

    This may sound unusual, but some people can deliberately imagine viewing themselves from a third-person perspective – as if watching the situation from the outside. When used intentionally and briefly, this can bring a new perspective and fresh insight into what's happening.

25. **Seek support focused on stability**

    Help that prioritises safety and functioning over persuasion works best.

26. **Allow insight to unfold**

    Many people later recognise these experiences as delusions – clarity usually follows stability, not force.

Skillset 11: Helpful Tips for Managing ADHD, Autism, and Dyslexia

Sometimes, when a client is having difficulty managing ADHD, autism, or dyslexia, I'll take a sheet of paper and draw a line down the middle. At the top of the first column, I write "Symptoms". At the top of the second, I write "Healthy ways of managing this". Because ADHD, autism, and dyslexia are, at their core, collections of symptoms that interfere with a person's life – this is literally the definition of the diagnosis.

Once we break things down this way, we can work on each symptom individually and look for practical solutions. The aim is to reduce the impact these symptoms have. From there, we start making a plan for how to apply these strategies in real life.

I often use myself as an example, because I have dyslexia. I know that I read slowly – but I comprehend what I'm reading very well. I know that my first draft of an email will usually contain a lot of errors. I know that reading numbers, especially things like telephone numbers, is genuinely difficult for me. And there are other things too.

So, if I'm attending a training, I let the trainer know that I have dyslexia. If there's reading involved, I explain that I may struggle to read it in the class, but I'll take it with me and read it later that evening – slowly, and in a quiet, distraction-free environment.

If I'm doing a test, I am given reasonable accommodations, such as extra time. When I send emails, I read over them carefully – and now I can also use AI to check them. When I read numbers, I slow right down and place my finger under each digit as I go.

These are simply the things I need to do to manage my dyslexia.

And importantly, dyslexia is not just something I manage – it's part of who I am. It's part of my way of navigating the world. It's part of my genius.

Sometimes I explain how I manage my own dyslexia as an introduction to this two-column worksheet. Then, week by week, we review each column together – learning more about the symptoms, how they affect the person, and which strategies genuinely help in their everyday life.

Here is an example of how someone can map their symptoms to helpful ways of managing them

My Personalised ADHD Support Map

What Can Be Hard with ADHD → A Helpful Support

- I forget what I planned to do or feel mentally scattered
  → Write down what I plan to do today and keep a simple, rough plan for the day

- Time disappears without me noticing
  → Set a reminder every two hours to look at my plan and gently reset

- My mind gets tired or overloaded
  → Take three short 5-minute mini-rests during the day

- My emotions become intense or overwhelming
  → Practise grounding skills that calm my body

and mind three times a day

- Big tasks feel impossible to start
  → Focus only on the very first step. Instead of thinking, "I have to write this email," think, "I need to open my email account." This elps get things started.

- I put things off because they feel too much
  → Break tasks down into small steps. Write them down if I need to, and focus on one step at a time, crossing them off as I go.

- I don't know what's helping or what isn't
  → Take a few minutes each night to reflect on how the day went. Over time, I'll spot patterns and see what helps me have a better day.

Living with ADHD can make everyday life feel harder than it should. Difficulties with attention, motivation, time management, organisation, impulse control, and emotional regulation are not personal failings – they are symptoms.

Many ADHD challenges, like procrastination, are overwhelm responses – not motivation problems. Strategies that help often focus on lowering the emotional load.

This approach is about working with your brain, rather than fighting it. These strategies are not about adding pressure to your brain, but taking pressure off.

Skillset 12: Ten Tips to Improve Emotional Self-Regulation

These tips are simple, practical ways to help you regain emotional stability in the moment and strengthen regulation over time.

1. **Slow the body first**

    Strong emotions are physiological. Slowing your breathing, relaxing your muscles, or grounding your body often reduces emotional intensity.

2. **Name what you're feeling**

    Quietly naming the emotion – anger, fear, shame, sadness – can reduce its grip. You're not analysing it, just taking a step back from it and acknowledging its presence.

3. **Reduce stimulation**

    When emotions escalate, reduce noise, screens, conversations, and decision-making. Emotional regulation improves when the nervous system has less to process.

If you can, move to a calm place. Choose gentle lighting, a pleasant scent, and relaxing surroundings.

4. **Buy time before responding**
You don't have to act immediately. Pausing – even briefly – often prevents doing something you may later regret and gives regulation a chance to return.

5. **Use the body to discharge emotion**
Walking, stretching, light physical tasks, or shaking out tension can help release emotional energy safely.

6. **Speak kindly to yourself**
What you say internally matters. Calm, reassuring self-talk ("This will pass," "I can handle this") supports regulation more than criticism.

7. **Lower expectations during emotional spikes**
When emotions are high, functioning temporarily drops. Adjusting expectations prevents secondary stress and shame.

8. **Return to something familiar and grounding**
   Routine activities – making tea, showering, tidying, listening to music – can stabilise the nervous system and restore balance.

9. **Reflect after the wave passes**
   Once regulated, gently notice what triggered the emotion and what helped. Learning happens after regulation, not during distress.

10. **Practice regulation when you're already okay**
    Skills strengthen through repetition. Practising grounding, breathing, and self-soothing when calm makes them easier to access when things are hard.

Emotional self-regulation isn't about control – it's about capacity: your capacity to deal with intense experiences. The more capacity you build, the less overwhelming emotions become, and the more choice you regain in how you respond.

Life is an emotional journey – and that's what makes it wonderful. Why would we want to close ourselves off from the full range of human emotion? All emotions have something to offer. They can inform us, motivate us, draw our attention to what matters, and help us grow. It's not the emotions themselves that cause harm, but how we react to them. When we walk the earth as conscious human beings, we realise that we can respond to our emotions in healthy or unhealthy ways – and we can choose the healthy ones.

Emotional self-regulation, then, isn't about limiting ourselves – it's about expanding our emotional lives.

So go for a walk in nature. Spend time with pets. Take slow, deep breaths to help your body process intense feelings. These simple acts create space, help you connect with and process your emotions, and allow you to experience life more fully, deeply, and richly.

Skillset 13: Ten Tips and One Exercise to Improve Your Thinking

Good thinking helps us live happier lives – lives where we can work toward our goals and dreams. Poor thinking, on the other hand, creates difficulty and can contribute to mental health and addiction struggles.

Our minds are like a garden, and the landscape of thoughts needs caring attention–gentle nurturing, thoughtful pruning, and the challenging of patterns that no longer serve us. When we tend to our thinking in this way, clarity grows, better choices become available, and what once felt out of reach becomes attainable.

Exercise

Highlight or underline the statements that resonate with you. When you notice yourself having an unhelpful thought, say the more helpful alternative out loud (or internally if others are around).

- Replace "What's wrong with me?" with "What might help right now?"

- Replace "This will never change" with "What's

one small thing I can do?"

- Replace "I can't cope" with "This is hard, and I can take it one step at a time."

- Replace "Why does this always happen?" with "What's actually happening right now?"

- Replace "I need to figure this out immediately" with "I can slow this down."

- Replace "I must know what will happen" with "I can tolerate not knowing for now."

- Replace "This is a disaster" with "This is difficult, but manageable."

- Replace "They must think badly of me" with "I don't actually know what they're thinking."

- Replace "I've messed everything up" with "What can I learn from this?"

- Replace "I can't stop thinking about this" with "I'll come back to this later."

- Replace "Something terrible is going to happen"

with "What's a more likely explanation?"

- Replace "I should be able to handle this" with "It's okay to need support."

- Replace "This feeling means something is wrong" with "Feelings rise and fall."

- Replace "I have to fix everything" with "What's within my sphere of influence right now?"

- Replace "I'm stuck like this" with "This is a moment, not a permanent state."

We are thinking healthily when we:

1. Take a few slow breaths before deciding what to do next.

2. Say to ourselves, "I don't quite know how to deal with this–and that's okay for now."

3. Choose reasonable explanations rather than worst-case scenarios.

4. Limit how long we dwell on the same thought.

5. Check whether our thinking is helping or harming us emotionally.

6. Recognise that sometimes what's needed isn't more thinking, but calmer thinking.

7. Shift our focus from what we can't change to what we can influence.

8. Ground our thinking in what's happening now, not what might happen later.

9. Write our thoughts down to gain clarity and perspective.

10. Share our thoughts with others and ask for their ideas or perspective.

Skillset 14: The Mood Thermometer

The Mood Thermometer is a practical tool to help you stay mindful throughout the day. It allows you to notice where you are emotionally and make adjustments when needed.

First, identify which zone you're in.
Then, decide how you want to respond.

The thermometer runs from **0 to 10**. You decide which aspect of your mood you want to track. For example, you might rate:

1. How negative or pessimistic your thinking and feelings are

2. How anxious you are feeling

3. How intense your symptoms of depression feel

4. How intense your cravings are

5. How intensely you are experiencing the symptoms of any diagnosis you currently have (for example, OCD)

6. How angry or irritable you are feeling

7. How overwhelmed you are feeling

The key is to customise the scale, so it measures something meaningful to you – something you want to work on over the coming days or weeks.

The Zones

Zone 1: No concern
0–1–2

You're doing well. Your mood is steady and not a concern.

Zone 2: Heating up
2–3–4–5

Your mood is noticeable but not overwhelming. It may be unhelpful and starting to make daily routines a little harder, but you're still functioning well.

Zone 3: Hot
5–6–7–8

Your mood is clearly getting in the way. Decision-making becomes harder, clear thinking is reduced, the risk of poor decisions increases, and everyday tasks take real effort. You can still push through using coping strategies – but it takes a lot of work.

Zone 4: Danger zone
8–9–10

This is the danger zone. Your mood is dominating your experience, severely impairing your ability to function and significantly increasing the risk of poor decisions. Daily tasks may feel impossible, and support is needed.

Using the Mood Thermometer: Three Phases

Using this tool typically moves through three phases.

- **Phase 1: Using it as an external tool for self-regulation**
  At first, you use the Mood Thermometer deliberately. You pause, look at the scale, review the zones, and decide where you are.

  You then choose how to respond. At this stage, it's helpful to have a written list of responses for each zone – simple actions you can refer to when needed. This supports intentional self-regulation and mindfulness.

- **Phase 2: Using it as an internalised tool for self-regulation**
  Over time, you no longer need to look at the thermometer. You can do a quick internal check and ask yourself, *"Which zone am I in?"*

  You'll also no longer need to refer to a written list. Through repetition, you become familiar with what works for you – you've built a mental toolkit.

- **Phase 3: Automatic self-regulation**

  In this phase, self-regulation becomes automatic. You're no longer consciously using a "tool" at all.

  Your mind has been trained through repetition. When your mood rises above Zone 1, helpful responses kick in automatically. And when you're in Zone 1, you naturally do things that help sustain it.

  At this point, self-regulation isn't something you do – it's simply a habit.

Don't get me wrong. I'm not saying that elevated levels of things like anxiety or anger are always bad. Sometimes these are appropriate and helpful responses–they can energise you and motivate you to take action.

So, for example, when you notice that you're in **Zone 2 for anger**, the response you choose might be: *yes, this anger makes sense–this feeling matters, it's valid.*

The key is mindfulness. It empowers you with choice: you get to decide how you want to respond.

So now, pick what you'd like to use the thermometer for. For example, it could be your level of anxiety, your level of anger, how intense your cravings are, or the intensity of symptoms of depression – such as feeling worthless, hopeless, having poor concentration, or low energy.

Exercise 1: Mapping the Zones

Take a little time to think about what each zone looks like for you.

You may find it helpful to write this down in two columns:

- Column 1: The zone
- Column 2: What you are thinking, feeling, and doing when you are in that zone

This can be a surprisingly insightful exercise.

Exercise 2: Choosing Your Responses

Next, write down the options you have for how to respond in each zone – practical steps you can take when you notice where you are.

This is a very individual process. The more you use the thermometer, the more developed and refined this list becomes, as you discover what works best for you.

Bringing It All Together

Use the Mood Thermometer to track whatever feels most relevant to you over the coming days or weeks. That could be anxiety, anger, low mood, cravings, or simply how overwhelmed you're feeling.

What matters isn't the label – it's how symptomatic you're feeling right now.

The purpose of the thermometer is simple: to help you function well throughout the day. It gives you a way to stay mindful of where you're at and to have practical steps you can take to move yourself to a better place when needed.

The scale runs from **0 to 10**. You can ask yourself, *"Where am I right now – from 0 to 10?"* or *"Which zone am I in?"*

At **0–1–2**, things are minimal. Whatever you're tracking is negligible and not really affecting your day. In this zone, the response may simply be to carry on – or to notice what you're doing that helps you stay here.

As you move into **2–3–4–5**, things become noticeable. Life is still manageable – you can function, work, and connect–but it takes more effort. Everything can feel a little more taxing. Here, you get to decide:

1. Do I need to take action now to reduce my score?

2. Is this something I can ride out?

3. Or are these healthy and appropriate feelings for this situation?

Maybe mornings are always rough for you and ease as the day goes on – so you tell yourself, *I just need to cope with this in a healthy way, and it will pass.* Or maybe you're coming home from work and don't want to stay in this state all evening–so you take deliberate steps to return yourself to Zone 1 and properly enjoy your evening. The decision is yours.

When you move into **5–6–7–8**, your mood is clearly interfering with life. Functioning becomes difficult, decision-making is harder, and you may be more prone to poor or risky choices. You can still get through the day–but it takes a lot of work and energy.

In this zone, taking corrective action really matters. You can look back over the other skills you've learned and choose what might help bring your score down. Sometimes the goal is simply to reduce your score by one point – often a very practical and achievable response.

Skills like emotional regulation, grounding, better thinking, or craving management need to be actively used here. This is where the time and energy you've put into learning the other skillsets really pays off.

As you move into **8–9–10**, life becomes unmanageable. Functioning breaks down. This is not a place to make decisions or engage in important conversations. The priority in this zone is safety, slowing down, and support.

You might decide in advance that when you reach this level, you won't make major decisions or have important conversations, you'll defer important actions, and you'll follow a pre-agreed plan – such as contacting specific people, reducing demands, going for a long walk in nature, or resting. This is highly individual, and over time you discover what works best for you.

The Mood Thermometer works best when you plan for these zones in advance. It also helps to plan for different environments, as your options may change depending on where you are. What helps at work may be different from what helps at home. Responses to the same zone can look different at different times of day too. Over time, you refine your plan as you learn what truly helps.

> **Suggestion:**
>
> Don't do this alone. Talk through your plans with others – a friend, a family member, a mentor, or a recovery professional – and develop steps and ideas together.
>
> This is a powerful way to increase your recovery capital by building connection and creating allies who support your recovery.
>
> Your friends and family are often eager to help, and this gives them a clear way in.

To recap:

At first, this is an external process. You use the thermometer visually. You write things down. You refer to your notes.

Then it becomes internalised. You can do a quick mental check-in – *Where am I right now?* – and you already know what helps.

Eventually, it becomes automatic. This way of self-regulating becomes part of how you move through the world. Not perfectly. Not all the time. But reliably enough to keep you functioning, grounded, and in a good place most of the time – confident that you can deal with whatever comes, because you've learned how to regulate your mood.

That's the goal.

The Mood Thermometer

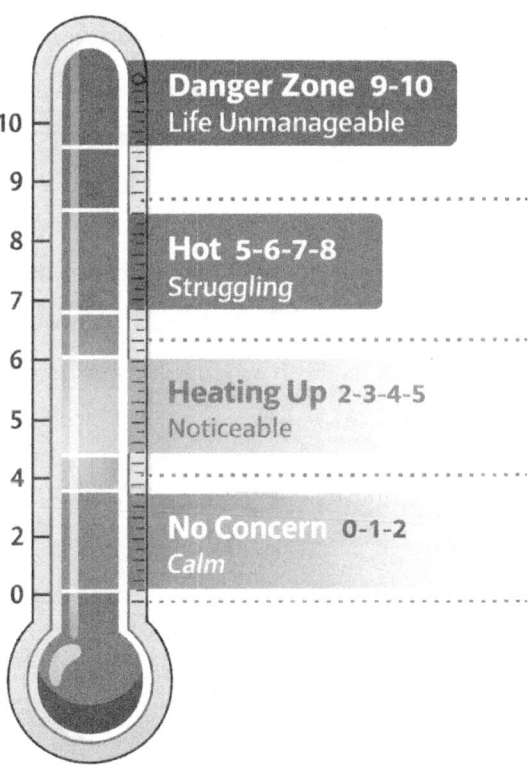

Skillset 15: Ask for Help Skillfully

Practical ways to reach out for support when you're struggling.

1. **Notice the early signs that you need support**
   Pay attention to changes in mood, sleep, cravings, anger, or stress. Asking early is always easier than waiting for a crisis.

2. **Identify safe people you can reach out to**
   This might be a friend, family member, counsellor, Recovery Peer, neighbour, teacher, or someone from a support group.

3. **Be clear about what you need**
   Instead of saying "I'm not coping," try something specific like:
   "Can we talk for ten minutes?"
   "I need help calming down."
   "I just need someone to listen."

4. **Keep it simple**
   You don't need to explain everything. A few honest sentences are enough.

5. Use "I" statements

"I'm struggling."
"I'm feeling overwhelmed."
"I need some support right now."
This keeps communication clear and non-blaming.

6. Ask for one thing

Keep the request small and doable – a chat, a walk, a lift, company, or advice. Small asks are easier for people to respond to.

7. Choose the right time and place

If possible, reach out when the person can give you their attention. If not, still ask – even a short moment of support helps.

8. Be honest about how you're feeling

You don't have to hide distress. Honest communication builds connection and understanding.

9. Try different methods of contacting someone

Phone, text, message, voice note, or in person – use whatever feels safest and easiest.

10. **Accept the help offered**
    Even if it's not perfect. Support often comes in small steps.

11. **Ask someone to sit with you while you calm down**
    You don't always need advice – sometimes a calm presence is enough.

12. **Reach out again if the first person can't help**
    This isn't a sign of rejection. People have their own limits. Keep going until you find someone who is available.

13. **Have a list of backup supports**
    Write down a few names and numbers – friends, helplines, groups, professionals – for times when you feel stuck.

14. **Practise asking for help when things are going well**
    Building the habit when you're calm makes it easier during difficult moments.

15. **Thank the person afterwards**

A simple "thank you" strengthens the connection and makes it easier to reach out next time.

Opening up is a process.
You don't have to do it all at once.
Bit by bit is fine.

Skillset 16: Harm Minimisation Skills

Practical ways to reduce risk if someone is still using.

1. **Use small amounts**
   The more you take, the greater the risk.

2. **Use in moderation**
   Avoid using everything at once – spread it out over time.

3. **Don't use alone**
   Have someone with you who is *not* using, so they can call for help if needed.

4. **Stick to one substance**
   Mixing drugs is dangerous because they can interact unpredictably.

5. **Don't use if you feel sleepy or exhausted**
   Tiredness increases the risk of overdose and accidents.

6. **Work toward using less**
   Connect with support to help you reduce gradually and safely.

7. **Start with a test dose**
When using illicitly, you can't know the strength or content. Use a very small amount first to see how it affects you.

8. **Seek help immediately if you feel unwell**
If anything feels wrong after using, call for help straight away.

9. **Avoid using illicit drugs on top of prescribed medication**
This increases the risk of overdose and other serious complications.

10. **Don't share equipment**
Sharing puts you at risk of infection and other harm.

11. **Be aware of the risks of falling asleep or becoming unconscious**
Using drugs can lead to fires, choking on vomit, severe burns, and other injuries. Moderation, avoiding mixing drugs, not using alone, and seeking help early all reduce risk.

12. **Remember that illicit drug use has unpredictable effects**

    People can injure themselves, fall, break bones, cut themselves, or behave in ways they regret. Each time you use, there are risks – do your best to use more safely.

13. **Connect with support**

    Talk with someone about your pattern of use and how to reduce harm.

The guidance provided here is general in nature and may not be suitable for everyone or every situation. Always seek professional guidance where there is a risk of harm.

Skillset 17: Making a Plan Skillfully

A good plan doesn't need to be detailed or perfect. In fact, the best plans are often **simple, flexible, and owned by the person themselves.** Your role is not to design their plan, but to help them shape one that feels realistic and supportive.

People are better off having some kind of plan, because it gives them something to reflect on and refine – week by week, or even day by day. Having no plan at all can leave someone feeling stuck or drifting for too long, and it can quietly steal the motivation, focus, and learning opportunities that come with having a plan. Helping them create their first plan – or even a loose structure, no matter how simple – is often a powerful step forward.

By skillfully helping your friend, family member, or loved one develop a plan, you support them to move forward with more clarity and confidence – without pressure, overwhelm, or taking control away from them.

Remember: they decide the goals and the steps. You're just helping out. **It's their plan – and that's the key.**

What Makes a Plan Helpful

A plan works best when it is:

- **Small** – focused on one or two steps, not everything at once

- **Collaborative** – talked through together, not imposed

- **Flexible** – able to change if it's not helping

- **Meaningful** – connected to what matters to *them*

- **Kind** – allows for off-days, pauses, and setbacks

If a plan feels heavy, rigid, or overwhelming, it usually needs simplifying.

How to Make a Plan Together

When the time feels right, you might gently explore:

- *"What feels like one small thing that could help this week?"*

- *"Is there anything you'd like to try, just as an experiment?"*

- *"What would make next week feel even one point better?"*

Listen carefully. Let their ideas lead. If they're unsure, you can offer **one** suggestion at a time – always with permission.

Keep the Plan Simple

A good plan often includes just three parts:

1. **One small step**
   Something doable, even on a hard day.

2. **When or how it might happen**
   Loose and flexible – not rigid or demanding.

3. **How you'll check in about it**
   A short conversation, a message, or a moment of reflection.

For example:

- A short walk together once this week

- Sending one message to someone supportive
- Trying one new coping skill once
- Making one appointment or enquiry
- Doing one small act of self-care

Small plans build confidence. Confidence builds momentum.

Plans Are Experiments – Not Tests

It can help to frame plans as **experiments**:

- There is no pass or fail
- Trying counts
- Learning matters more than outcomes

Afterwards, gently reflect together:

- *"How did that feel?"*
- *"Was it helpful, neutral, or not helpful?"*
- *"Would you want to keep it, tweak it, or drop it?"*

If something didn't help, that's useful information – not a failure.

> Sometimes, after our first session, a client will tell me that the plan didn't work – for example, they may have drunk even more than usual that week. They're often relieved when I tell them that this doesn't mean anything has gone wrong, and that it's actually quite common.
>
> What matters is not whether the plan worked perfectly, but that we're going to talk about what happened and learn from it. That conversation – gaining insight together – is success for that session.
>
> I explain that it's common for the first plan we make not to work straight away. It was only our first attempt. We tried something, and now we've learned something. That's how progress happens.

I'll often say something like, "You tried it – good on you. That's a great approach to your recovery. Because trying, reflecting, and adjusting is real progress.

Watch for Overload

If you notice any of these signs, it may be time to scale back:

- Increased anxiety or avoidance

- A sense of pressure or obligation

- Guilt for not following the plan perfectly

- Withdrawal or shutdown

When this happens, return to basics.

One small step for the week.
One short conversation about the plan.
The rest of the time, focus on being present, supportive, and understanding.

Respect Pace and Readiness

Not every week is a planning week.

Sometimes the most helpful plan is:

- Rest

- Stabilisation
- Connection
- Simply getting through the week safely

Trust the pace. Recovery is not a race.

And naturally, as people grow stronger in their recovery, they often begin to want more structure and gently more challenging steps to support further progress.

Your Role in the Plan

Your role is to:

- Offer steadiness
- Ask open questions that allow them to explore their experience
- Reflect what you hear
- Encourage learning
- Stay flexible

You are not managing their recovery. You are contributing – accepting the ups and downs as they come, and adjusting your approach to what fits and feels supportive. Sometimes this can feel tricky – and it is – but this is one of the core skills we develop as helpers. It takes reflection, practice, and mindfulness to develop, and it's worth it when we see the people we care about benefit from that skillfulness over time.

A plan that belongs to them will always work better than a plan that looks good on paper.

Even the smallest plan moves recovery forward one step at a time.

4 Keys to Unlock Your Recovery Potential

Recovery becomes far more likely when these four simple questions are answered:

1. **What skills** are you going to tap into and develop?

2. **What strengths** are you going to build on?

3. **What supports** are you going to connect with?

4. **What resources** are available to you right now?

But here's the key that unlocks the power of all four: You must engage with these skills, strengths, supports, and resources in a way that is **meaningful and engaging to you**—transforming them from what *should* work into what *does* work for you.

And there's one final step that **secures** all of this: **Measure your progress.**

Tracking your progress helps you spot early warning signs when things start slipping or when you're getting stuck–*before* you fall off track. That way, you can make some adjustments early and keep moving forward.

This is what turns recovery from a hope into a reality.

Chapter Five

Advice from 20 Years of Experience

My Guiding Mantra

Every day, as I go to work and help people recover from a wide range of mental health, addiction, and trauma-related concerns, there is one sentence – one guiding principle – that I return to constantly: *I can't fix, cure, or save anybody, but I can always humbly contribute to their recovery capital.* That's what I focus on. I developed this mantra many years ago to help me stay sane in this work, and I now find it invaluable.

The irony is that, through this process, people often do get "fixed." The problem that brought them to counselling no longer troubles them. Many are "cured" – old pains heal and past demons fall silent. And people are even "saved" – from harmful paths that once felt inevitable.

But none of this is ever my aim in a session, in a moment, or on any given day. I don't orient myself around fixing, curing, or saving people. I focus on the process that matters most – the one that maximises the likelihood of recovery. That is my job, and it's one I have spent over twenty years learning how to do better.

> *You can't fix, cure, or save anybody – but you can always humbly contribute to their recovery capital.*

Now, don't misunderstand me. If someone is at immediate risk of serious harm, that always comes first. It is addressed openly, safety plans are put in place, others are involved when needed, and I consult closely with colleagues.

So when you're with your friend, family member, or loved one, keep this principle in mind. And when you're thinking about them in their absence, look at the situation through this lens – you'll often find yourself inspired with new, ever more helpful ways of supporting them.

When you talk with others who care about them and want to help, share this mantra. Use it as a common framework. Together, you'll come up with ideas that help your friend or family member take their next step in building recovery capital–steps that are meaningful to them, taken at a pace that works for them, and shaped into a plan that fits where they are right now.

Maybe the first time you ask yourself the question, *"How can I contribute to their recovery capital?"*, you'll come up blank. That's okay. Stay with the question. Reflect on it often. Over time, ideas will begin to come.

You might find yourself:

- Sending a brief, thoughtful text
- Meeting them for a coffee
- Encouraging them to keep going
- Suggesting resources they might want to explore
- If something feels overwhelming for them, ask if

they'd like you to come along for support.

- Suggesting they consider using something to measure their progress – and briefly explaining how that works, so they know it's an option

- Sharing one of the skill-building sheets from this book, and helping them use it

Keep asking the right question: *"How can I help them build their recovery capital in a way that feels positive and supportive for them?"*

Trust me – the answers will come.

It's Not a Sprint

Sometimes a client's life is improving. Sometimes they're in crisis. Sometimes unexpected things happen that set them back. Through all of that, I stay steady. This isn't a sprint – it's a marathon. I aim to be an anchor, a steady beat in their life that they can rely on. When someone is in crisis, they don't need the people supporting them to be overwhelmed as well. They need to know that the person beside them is doing okay – and *has it together*.

This isn't about being cold or detached. It's about being the best support you can be. Empathy matters. It's important to feel, to some degree, the pain, struggle, and distress they're experiencing. That human connection is essential. But it's just as important to have a little distance. That distance helps you stay balanced, see things in perspective, and offer calmer, steadier support – because that's what they need.

Sometimes, in the moment, you need to pause and take a breath to ground yourself. Sometimes you need to step away from the situation to orient yourself again. That's not failure – it's part of being a reliable support.

I'm not sprinting. I'm in this for the long haul. I stay consistent. I'm a regular presence – someone they can count on, with healthy boundaries that make this possible. I stay with people through the ups and downs, letting them know it's okay to have better days and difficult days – and that I'm okay with that. I'm glad they're talking to me. Glad we're working on this together. Glad we're figuring things out as we go, and occasionally looking back to learn a few lessons along the way. I encourage you to take the same approach with the people you love. When you do, you really are doing everything you can.

Many of the people I work with are, at times – as we'd say in Ireland – *all over the place*. They don't need me to join them there. I listen. We set meaningful goals. We talk about how things are going. We adjust the plan when it's not working. We measure progress. And they know I'm not going anywhere. I'm here. Steady. With them.

Don't Go It Alone

Another thing I use all the time as a professional – and something I strongly encourage you to invest time in developing – is a network of people who can support you. This might include professionals you can talk things through with, other people who have supported loved ones through mental health or addiction difficulties, or people in your life who haven't dealt with any of this but are simply wise, thoughtful, and help you think and feel more clearly about whatever situation you're facing.

I'm always talking to colleagues about the people I support and how best to help them. They talk to me about their clients too. Sometimes this happens one-to-one; other times I bring a situation to the whole team and ask for ideas, perspective, and support. New insights nearly always emerge.

Knowing that this support is there makes a huge difference. I know my colleagues are there for me. If I'm worried that I'm not doing the right thing, or that I haven't given my best, they can offer guidance and reassurance. When I ask the team for support, I get a range of perspectives to consider. And just as importantly, they're there for me emotionally – as I am for them. This is emotional work, and we all need an emotional support crew.

At times, I can feel overwhelmed with worry for a client who's at risk. Sometimes I'm riddled with doubt about whether I'm doing enough or even the right thing. Sometimes I'm deeply affected and upset by the struggles I see people going through. That's why everyone on the team knows that the others are there for them when the emotional weight of the work builds up. And it works. These are good people – great to talk to when you're struggling emotionally. Often, they know exactly what to say, and sometimes they know that all they need to do is listen. After all, that's what they do professionally.

You need that kind of network around you too. Friends you can talk openly with. People who may have more experience with recovery. Sometimes professionals as well. And you might be surprised – we often love sharing what we've learned over the years. In fact, we may even bore you to death if you don't stop us once we get started.

This network isn't there to tell you what to do. It's there to offer ideas, share perspectives, help you think things through, and offer emotional support – letting you know that you are not in this alone. Sometimes that's exactly what you need to take the next step forward in supporting the people you care most about.

Find Your Style

One of the wisest things we learn as professionals is that everyone has a different style. I work with people in a certain way. Other professionals work with people in their own way. That's exactly why we often encourage people to have more than one source of support. Someone may benefit from my particular strengths, while also gaining something different from a group facilitator, a psychiatrist, a mentor, or a peer supporter. Each person brings something unique, and together those differences add up.

What matters most, though, is that you will develop your own style for helping someone recover. You don't have to do it the way anyone else does. Bring your strengths. From time to time, reflect on what those are – patience, commitment, wisdom, calmness, perceptiveness, positivity, energy, steadiness. There's no prescribed way you have to be. The question isn't always *"What should I do?"* Sometimes it's *"What's my approach to this?"* What's your way of being there for them? What's your way of keeping healthy boundaries? What's your style of talking about progress, offering support during setbacks, helping them think things through, and supporting them to build new skills?

Just allow yourself to say: *This is my style.*

I work alongside colleagues every day, and each of us has a different way of working with people – and that's a good thing. Our fundamentals are the same: building therapeutic relationships and strong working alliances; paying attention to progress; helping people connect with helpful supports and resources. These are the same fundamentals

I encourage you to use in this book – just without the jargon. But as professionals, our approaches differ. I'm not there to tell a colleague what their style should be. I'm there to understand it, support it, and sometimes help them develop what's unique about the way they work. And at times, I'm there to help them strengthen the fundamentals too – because even experienced people can find those challenging at times.

The same applies to you. Reflect on your style. Develop it. Lean into your strengths, and build new ones over time. You don't need to get this perfect – just aim to be good enough. Give yourself a break. You're doing your best, and that's all anyone can ask. And if something goes wrong, return to the basics, make sure they're solid, and rely on your support network.

I learn something about recovery from every person I help. Simply by showing up and doing your best, you're already growing – becoming wiser, more capable, and more attuned to the individual way you support the people you care about.

You don't have to be perfect. You just need to find an approach that works for both you and them. That's your style – uniquely yours. It's the steady presence you bring, shaped by who you are, your values, and how you show up when it matters. And often, that quiet consistency is far more powerful than any technique.

And perhaps more than this, it's something deeper too. It's your presence in the world – your unique way of being – something no one else can replicate or replace. A radiance that is yours alone. A gift only you can give.

When we give ourselves fully to this work, we don't just help others change – we change too. And somehow, in ways we can't always explain, forces beyond our understanding come to our aid when we need them most – even if, at times, it's hard to see.

Chapter Six

Enabling, Crisis, and Critical Situations — How to Respond Well

Avoid Enabling

Someone you care about has an addiction, and you're trying to support them through it. Along the way, you've probably heard the word *"enabling"* – and you may be worried that you're doing it without realising.

Let's start by being clear about what enabling actually means.

Enabling occurs when you are doing one or both of the following:

1. **Helping the person gain access to the object of their addiction,** directly or indirectly.

2. **Reducing or removing the consequences of their addiction** in a way that makes continued use easier or more likely.

That's it.
Enabling isn't about kindness or intention – it's about the effect.
It's the unintended negative effect of our efforts to help.

To fully understand enabling, we also need a practical definition of addiction.

An addiction is a behaviour that a person continues despite it causing significant harm to their life. This harm may show up in one or more areas, such as:

- Close relationships

- Physical or mental wellbeing
- Finances
- Housing
- Legal standing
- Employment or education

People can be addicted to many things, including drugs, alcohol, pornography, online shopping, and gambling.

Now that we understand things more clearly, you are better equipped to distinguish between support that genuinely helps and support that unintentionally keeps the problem going.

Often this distinction is clear, but sometimes it can be trickier to figure out. And that's OK – I'll guide you through a process to help find the path.

For example, you may pay off some of the debts that have developed through their addiction, with the intention of helping them move forward or avoiding harm if the debt remains unpaid. This can be a critical situation and emotionally very difficult, especially when you see someone you love at risk of real harm.

But once you've paid it off, they're right back using. And this brings us to the heart of what addiction is. Most often – at least after a little time – the person knows that their addiction is causing harm and emotional pain. If this weren't an addiction, they would make changes. They might become more moderate in their use, or stop altogether. And that happens all the time when people don't have an addiction.

I was speaking to a client once and told her that, at a certain point, I realised I was drinking a little too much. Pretty much every evening, I was drinking four cans of moderately strong beer (3.4 percent alcohol), and a little more at the weekend. I'd been doing this for about six months.

I told the client, that one day I mentioned it to a friend. It wasn't a heavy conversation – I just brought it up casually and was curious about her opinion. She said, *"Yeah, that's probably not good for you."*

And I thought to myself, *Yeah – this isn't good for me.*

You see, I had slowly slipped into this pattern. It started with a few beers at the weekend – moderate drinking, often with food – and maybe one evening during the week as well. It was nice. Relaxing. Pleasant. So I thought, *Why not have it on a few more evenings?* And that was nice too. Before long, I was having four beers every night – and enjoying them.

But after that conversation, I reviewed the situation and said, OK – time to cut back. It wasn't a big deal. I just skipped drinking on a few evenings each week, spent my time on other, more productive activities, and engaged more with hobbies and interests.

Within a few months, I was back to having just a few cans at the weekend.

So I told this story to the client, just to explain how different people can have very different relationships with alcohol.

She was drinking gin every evening. She knew it wasn't good for her, but she wasn't able to change it. She wasn't doing anything productive with her time – she drank alone, and sometimes drank to excess, leaving her with a hangover at work the next day.

During the day, she would find herself thinking obsessively about how nice it will be to drink that evening. And every workday, the first thing she did when she got home was start drinking. She would sip her gin throughout the evening, right up until she put her head down to drift off to sleep.

When I explained my experience of cutting back, she was genuinely amazed that someone could do that. She'd tried, at times, not to drink in the evening, or to delay drinking until after 7 p.m., but it was always hard work – and it never lasted.

This was helpful, as she realised her relationship with alcohol was compulsive. Even though she wanted to stop because of its negative impact on her life, she couldn't.

That is a core aspect of addiction. It's compulsive. And it's often obsessive, preoccupying a person's thinking. It's helpful for people who don't struggle with that compulsion to understand what it's like.

At the heart of healing from addiction is helping someone overcome that compulsion. I've helped thousands of people do exactly this, and shortly I'll explain how it's done.

So, with this in mind, let's return to the story of the person who went straight back to using once the debts were paid off. They didn't want to fall into debt again. They didn't want to be in danger again. And they didn't want to betray the kindness that had been shown to them. But the compulsion and obsession of addiction simply kicked back in.

The person who paid off the debts is left feeling hurt, wondering whether they've really helped at all. The debt was cleared, the immediate danger averted – but it's all likely going to happen again.

Then, two months later, it has. They're in debt again, and back in danger if it isn't paid soon. They're distressed, feeling trapped between their compulsion to use and the devastating impact it's having on their life. They reach out for help, asking again for the debt to be paid.

But now, the person who paid it off the first time is confused. They don't want harm to come to someone they care about – but they also don't want to facilitate continued use. They don't want to enable the addiction.

So, the first thing I need to say is this: it's often not easy to figure this out when you're first faced with a situation like this. That's normal.

I'll walk you through the steps you need to take.

First, slow down.
Talk with one or two trusted friends about your predicament. Take some time to think it through. Then, instead of reacting in the moment, develop the best plan you can to support the person you care about.

Second, think about your safety.
Develop healthy boundaries and maintain them. Review your boundaries from time to time too. Remember, this is key to helping effectively. I covered this in the first chapter.

Third, consider your own wellbeing.
Make sure you have people around you who can support you emotionally.

Fourth, develop a plan that helps you to:

1. Help them be safer.

2. Help them build recovery capital.

3. Avoid enabling, where addiction is a concern.

No plan is perfect. And you're not aiming for that – you're aiming for *good enough*. You're not saving them, because you can't do that. And that can be hard to accept, especially when you desperately want to save them. But when you do accept this, you're ready to mindfully help them move toward recovery and greater safety, without enabling.

But I can't. Sometimes, that's how I feel about my clients. I want to save them. But I can't. I pour that passion into humbly and mindfully helping them move toward recovery. I recognise that I only have a certain degree of influence over the situation, and I do my best to focus on and take care of that. I also know that if I try to do more than this, I may end up being less helpful – or even doing harm.

When you follow the three steps outlined above – which I'll go into in more detail shortly – you can find peace knowing that you're doing your very best to help the person you love.

Tips to Help You Develop Your Plan

Tip 1: You don't have to figure this out by yourself.
Talk with trusted friends and family members, and others who care about the person you're trying to support. Consider joining a support group for friends and family of people with addiction – it can be a safe place to talk things through and hear how others have handled similar situations.

You might also consider attending educational programmes, which can offer new perspectives and practical ideas. Talking with people who are in recovery – who are no longer using – can be especially helpful, as they can offer insights from lived experience. And speaking with professionals in the field can provide guidance and clarity.

When I'm working with clients and I'm not sure how best to proceed – and even after 20 years of doing this, that still happens frequently – I turn to my colleagues. I'll bring the situation to a team meeting and draw on the wisdom and experience of others to help me think things through.

I'm not asking them to tell me what to do. I'm asking for insights, options, and help processing the situation so I can develop the sound plan.

That support is essential to me. And I strongly suggest you develop your own network of people who can support you too.

Tip 2: Focus on creating a healthy process around a challenging problem.
Many times, the critical problems that clients bring to me aren't ones I can address directly. I can't see a simple path where they can just be "fixed." So rather than focusing on the problem itself, I focus on the process.

I ask myself two questions:

- **How can I collaborate with them to help them be safer right now?**

- **How can we use this situation as an opportunity to build recovery capital?**

Because, ultimately, building recovery capital is the way out – the path to safety and recovery.

So I focus on two things: helping them be safer in the present, and supporting their movement toward recovery over time. When both of those are happening, they are moving forward.

From there, it becomes about discussing these two aims with the client and breaking them down into practical, achievable steps.

Let me give an example. In my first session with a client, he explained that he'd been using heroin daily after inheriting £30,000 when his grandmother died a year earlier. The money was now gone, but he couldn't stop using. He was getting into a lot of debt and was scared.

After listening carefully for about 40 minutes to his story, his feelings, and his distress, I told him he wasn't alone – and that we'd work on this together.

I explained that, ultimately, the only path to safety was abstinence, and that I'd help him get there – that it was possible. I also told him that we'd need to work out a way to deal with the debt, but that if he continued using, he'd never escape it.

The key was that what I said made sense to him. I'd taken the time to really listen and understand what he was going through, and he believed me when I told him I could help – and that it was possible.

So he came up with a plan to pay some of the debt off, giving himself some time. He agreed to see me twice a week while the situation was critical, and to connect with other supports. He began attending groups, learning new skills, and learning how to open up and talk about himself.

He also connected with services that help people manage debt. And week by week, we worked through things together.

A few months later, he was no longer using – with occasional lapses that we processed and learned from. A year later, he had a job and had almost paid his debts off.

And I think the key to all of this is that I wasn't doing it alone. I wasn't the only one helping him be safer and move toward recovery. Other professionals were involved. People who were in recovery themselves helped along the way.

In effect, there was a team supporting him. And most of the time, that's exactly what a person needs to recover – a network of support that helps them find safety again.

While I was working with him, especially in the first few months, I was concerned about his safety. I discussed his situation in supervision and with colleagues, doing my best to plan how I could support him to be safer and progress in recovery.

I think the word "safer" is important. When people are in addiction, there is always risk. There is no safe way to be in addiction – it is harmful by its very nature.

But there are almost always ways to be safer. And I've found that people in addiction, even if they don't yet want to stop, are often willing to talk about things they can do to reduce risk and be safer.

And it's important to say this clearly: even when a person doesn't want to stop using, we can still help them progress in recovery.

That might sound strange, but it's true.

When a client tells me they don't want to stop, or that they don't believe they have a problem, I don't argue with them. I simply help them move forward anyway.

The fact that they're talking to me matters – it's a building block for recovery, whether they see it that way or not. They're processing what's happening in their life. They may be open to a few new ideas. They might be willing to meet someone who's in recovery. They're connecting with support regularly. They may also be working on other goals – perhaps homelessness is an issue, or there's a health concern that needs attention.

Over time, I become someone they can trust and open up to. And relationships like that can be exactly what's needed at the very beginning of a person's journey toward recovery.

All of this is positive. All of this is adding up, strengthening the foundations of recovery in a way that works for them, at a pace they can accept, in a way that feels positive to them.

And then, often over time, they become tired of the damage their addiction is causing. When that happens, a door opens – and we can begin talking about bringing it to an end.

Tip 3: Build a team around them.
One of the best things I can do to help people recover is encourage them to connect with others who can support and assist them. That might involve pointing them toward other resources or professionals who can help with specific concerns.

It often means linking them with peer support groups, connecting them with recovery mentors, and helping them find the words to bring friends and family on board – so those people can become allies in supporting their recovery.

I was with a client once, and he asked me a simple question: How is recovery actually done?

So I asked him if he knew who Steve-O was from the Jackass movies. He said he did, and that he knew Steve-O had struggled with addiction and was now in recovery – free from drugs and alcohol.

I told him that I'd once watched a video where Steve-O was asked the very same question: How is it done? Steve-O's answer was simple. Just two words: "Mod up."

Steve-O went on to explain that by this he meant to connect with people who are in recovery. Spend time with them. Make new friends. They're your people now – your crew.

That's how it's done.

To be honest, I wasn't sure how he would take the story. But I thought it might really strike a chord with him. And if it hadn't, I would have simply moved on and found another way to explain it.

But it did strike a chord with him. He talked about it a lot – how much sense it made to him – and he said he was all in for doing it this way.

So we developed practical steps, week by week, for how to do exactly that. And it worked for him. He grew. He learned. He made new friends. He found a place where he had a team supporting him – and where he, in turn, was able to support others.

Not overnight, and not without challenges. But with time, he found sobriety – and, believe it or not, something people in addiction often tell me they want more than anything else: a normal life.

So when someone you care about is in a critical situation – whether due to addiction or a mental health concern – one of the best things you can do is help them connect with a range of supportive people, all working to help them be safer and make progress.

It takes the pressure off you. You're not the only one trying to help them be safer – and that brings peace of mind. It's not all on you. The load is shared. A team of people is supporting them, and often supporting one another too.

Support at Critical Moments

Here is a story where I helped someone through a period of elevated risk, while also using it as an opportunity to strengthen their recovery – so that afterwards, they were in a much better place.

When I started working with this client, she was drinking twice a week and getting blackout drunk. After about two months, she had a few weeks of abstinence under her belt. And then she relapsed.

By coincidence, we had a session scheduled for the next day, in the afternoon. Had it been a morning appointment, I doubt she would have made it.

So we processed what had happened. I told her I was glad she'd come to the session, and that talking about it and gaining insight was the right thing to do. I also explained that, for many people, relapses and lapses are part of the process – they're still learning how to live without alcohol.

About halfway through the session, she said she was worried. When she got up that morning to take her mental health medication, the box was empty. She didn't remember taking it, but assumed she must have taken all the tablets the night before.

She wasn't having thoughts of suicide. But because she couldn't remember what had happened the night before, she believed she must have taken them.

I took a moment to think it through. Then I asked what the medication was, how much was in each tablet, and how many she believed she'd taken. I opened my laptop and looked it up to see whether this was a dangerous amount.

It was.

I explained some of the symptoms she was likely to experience over the next 24 hours, such as agitation and restlessness. I also told her that it was strongly advised she go to A&E for observation.

She called a taxi to take her there. While we waited, I suggested it would be a good idea to ask a friend or family member to meet her at A&E and support her over the next few hours. She was hesitant, but I gently encouraged her.

We met again a week later. She said they'd kept her in for 12 hours for observation, and that she'd been OK.

She also told me that her brother and best friend had come to see her, and that they were very supportive. Opening up to them about her drinking suddenly felt possible – she realised she could talk to them about it now.

She'd also been referred to the hospital mental health team, who were offering follow-up support, which I strongly encouraged her to engage with.

A Critical Boundary

A mother whose son was addicted to heroin and crack sought my help. She didn't feel safe having him in her home, as at times he became violent and abusive when he needed money for drugs. She had tried to get help and to reach some kind of agreement that might prevent it. But it kept happening. She was overwhelmed and completely depleted.

So I listened. I let her tell her story, and I gave her space to offload some of the stress she'd been carrying. Then I said that she needed to put some clear boundaries in place. We agreed that her son could no longer stay in her home, and that if he refused to leave, she would call the police. The police had been called before when he became violent. She also decided that she would no longer give him money, as it was only being used to buy drugs.

So she set two clear boundaries – and, just as importantly, we talked through how she would maintain them.

Then I encouraged her to think about how she could continue to support him once those boundaries were in place. She said she would do anything she could – so we came up with some ideas. She decided she could meet him for a meal in a restaurant twice a week. She felt that meeting earlier in the day would be safer, and choosing a busy restaurant helped her feel more secure. She also agreed that she would let someone know where she was going and when she expected to be back, and that she would call them afterwards to let them know she'd returned safely. We also made a clear plan for what that person would do if she didn't make that call.

She also said she would be happy to help her son organise appointments and connect with support. So when they met, she brought a planner and had researched options that might help him – including housing support, as he was now homeless, as well as recovery supports he could choose to engage with, or at least be aware of.

She also said she would begin attending a support group for family members of people with addiction.

I advised her to have someone with her when she told her son about these boundaries, and to choose a time when he was more likely to receive it well. I encouraged her to be calm and clear when explaining them, and not overly emotional during the conversation.

She wasn't arguing or negotiating – she was simply giving him information about what the situation would be going forward.

Her son accepted the terms. He said, he had been expecting it.

She was no longer enabling his use. She felt safe. And she knew she was doing all she could to help her son. It wasn't an easy situation – and it was only one step in a much longer journey of supporting him toward recovery.

And she was now receiving emotional support, practical suggestions, and a place to process her thoughts through the support group.

There are many different critical situations you may need to support someone through when addiction or a mental health concern is present, including:

- Dangerous patterns of use
- Self-harm

- Suicidal ideation

- Reckless spending

- Risky sexual behaviour

- Violent situations, including periods of increased risk of being assaulted, exploited, or taken advantage of while using

After more than two decades working in this field, I've supported people through all of these situations. And I can tell you – it isn't easy. It's always challenging, both practically, in terms of figuring out how best to help, and emotionally, in terms of carrying the weight of it.

But it's also rewarding work. And when a critical situation passes, there's often a deep sense of relief and accomplishment. Very often, going through a moment like this helps a person move a little further along their journey toward recovery.

I have also worked with a small number of clients who didn't make it. Just a few – a number I can count on one hand. I remember each of them. I remember their stories. I wish them peace now, wherever they are.

And I take solace in knowing that I did all I could. Truly – I did all I could.

I carry that knowledge with me as I continue this work, aware that while a few didn't make it, most have. And I remain committed to helping many more people find recovery, begin a new chapter in their lives, and positively impact the lives of those around them.

Chapter Review: Responding Well in Critical Situations

- **First, slow down.**
  Give yourself time to think rather than reacting in the moment.

- **Second, think about your safety.**
  Put clear boundaries in place to protect yourself, and maintain them.

- **Third, consider your own wellbeing.**
  Make sure you have emotional support and space to process what's happening.

- **Fourth, develop a plan that helps you to:**
  1. Help them be safer
  2. Support progress toward recovery
  3. Avoid enabling, where addiction is a concern

Connect with others who can support you emotionally and help you think the situation through.

Focus on the process, not just the problem. Ask yourself:

How can I collaborate with them to help them be safer right now?

How can this situation be used to support progress toward recovery?

Build a team around them.

Don't try to do this alone.

Important: When there are significant risks to safety – such as self-harm or suicidal ideation – professional support is essential. In these situations, the priority is immediate safety. If you're unsure how to respond, contact emergency services or local crisis support.

Chapter Seven

Dealing with Guilt, Shame, and Regret

It's natural to ask ourselves, *Could I have done something different?*

We replay the past, look for mistakes we made, and search for moments where things might have turned out differently. That's human nature. It's because we care so deeply.

Feelings of guilt and regret are part of this process—an unavoidable part of the inner journey. At times, they can feel devastating. But they are not something to run from or suppress. They are part of the process we must learn to move through, rather than avoid.

Because you're reading this book, I want you to hear something clearly: **this is not your fault.** You are not to blame. This is not something you chose–it's something that happened. Knowing this matters.

Beating yourself up with guilt, regret, or endless *what ifs* doesn't help. *Could I have done better? What did I do wrong?* These questions come easily in hindsight, but they are unfair ones.

At the time, with the insight, information, and emotional resources you had, you did the best you could. That's what people do. That's what we all do. It's all any of us can do.

Yes, looking back, it's often possible to see how things might have been handled differently. But that perspective only exists now. Back then, you were doing the best you could in that moment.

And even if mistakes were made–because you're human–it still doesn't mean you are to blame. Being human means being imperfect.

So reflect on the past—without slipping into rumination or dwelling on it in an unhealthy way. Reflecting in a healthy way allows us to learn and grow.

When we review these events, feelings of guilt, shame, and regret are natural. Don't beat yourself up with them. Instead, allow them to motivate you in a positive way: to do the best you can now. That is the path of healing—the path of self-acceptance and self-forgiveness.

Rather than turning against yourself, respond to these feelings by saying: I may have made mistakes in the past. Maybe I could have done more. But at the time, I did the best I could.

What you choose to take from the past is not self-blame or self-punishment, but learning. Not feeling bad about yourself, but allowing yourself to be motivated—to do your best now, with what you know today.

This is how we grow and learn from the past without harming ourselves along the way.

What is the best you can do now?

The guidelines in this book are designed to give you a framework for answering that question.

The best you can do now is to maintain healthy boundaries and take care of yourself and your own safety. The best you can do now is to contribute–humbly and realistically–to their recovery capital.

That may mean helping them stay a degree safer. It may mean helping them connect with new resources. It means being a steady support–listening, being present, believing in them, offering encouragement, sharing new skills, or gently introducing the idea of tracking progress. It often means encouraging others to become involved, so this isn't carried alone.

And most importantly, develop a network of supportive people to support you.

When you do these things, you are doing the best you can for the person you love. And that is all that any of us can do.

Because ultimately, we don't get to control the outcome. We only get to do the best we can to make a positive outcome more likely. That's simply the truth of it.

Heal the past through how you relate to the present. For how can we heal others if we don't first look to heal ourselves?

> **Key Takeaway**
>
> Looking back and questioning yourself is a natural part of caring deeply about others. Guilt, shame, and regret are human responses – not signs of failure. What matters is learning to reflect without rumination, to separate human imperfection from blame, and to treat yourself with the same understanding you would offer someone you love.
>
> You cannot change the past, but you can choose how you respond now – by caring for yourself, setting healthy boundaries, and contributing, realistically and compassionately, to the recovery journeys of others. That is enough.
>
> You can be proud of yourself, because you are growing and learning so you can better support the people you love.

> And you can be proud of yourself for having the courage it takes to do this inner work.

Chapter Eight

Be Honest, Genuine and Truthful

Genuineness matters. When people know you genuinely care and are truly there for them, it has impact.

In my work with clients, I believe this is the most important thing – as long as the client feels that I genuinely care about them, everything else can be figured out. From this foundation, my role is to stay curious, understand their situation, and offer ideas they experience as helpful.

Be honest, not brutal. Be tactful and wise as you speak with honesty. The people we love deserve honesty. They deserve to know when we are genuinely concerned or worried about them. Silence, avoidance, or pretending everything is fine often does more harm in the long run.

Honesty delivered without care can wound, shame, or push someone further away.

Honesty delivered with compassion can strengthen trust and deepen connection.

Being honest means:

- Speaking truthfully
- Being thoughtful and tactful
- Choosing timing and context carefully

Expressing Concern Without Causing Harm

When someone is making choices that are clearly harming them, it's reasonable – and necessary – to say something. The challenge is how to express concern without offending, shaming, or creating distance.

The key is intention and framing:
You're not speaking to control them.

You're not speaking to win an argument.
You're speaking because you care.

That difference matters.

You might say:

- *"I'm saying this because I care about you."*
- *"I might be wrong, but I'm worried about you."*
- *"I don't want to judge – I just want to be honest about what I'm seeing."*

You can ask someone to listen.
You can share your concern.
But beyond that, you must accept that their choices are ultimately theirs.

That acceptance isn't approval – it's reality. And this acceptance allows you to stay with them, continuing to offer support and when they're open to it, guidance.

So today, they didn't accept what I said – but they heard it. They may change their mind later. For now, I've said my piece, and I'll leave it at that.

And you are letting them know that you are OK with their response, that you not trying to control them – because you are wise enough to know you can't.

In time, they may change their mind and become more open to your advice. There's wisdom in keeping this in mind.

When Choices Are Risky

If someone you care about is making risky or unsafe choices, your role is not to force change, but to reduce harm where possible.

If they are going to continue using substances, you can offer guidance about safer use.

If they are entering unsafe situations, you can encourage steps that reduce the risk of a negative outcome.

If they are emotionally overwhelmed, you can suggest grounding, support, and staying in safer environments until they are more settled and able to make better choices.

And if there is a **serious risk of significant harm to themselves or others**, it's important to be clear: involving emergency services or professional help is not a betrayal. It is an act of care.

Safety always comes first.

The Courage to Have Hard Conversations

Often, the conversations we most want to avoid are the ones that matter most.

Hard, emotional, honest conversations can:

- Break down walls
- Open doors
- Reset relationships
- Create turning points

But they require courage – and insight.

A difficult conversation should strengthen recovery capital, not undermine it. If honesty leaves someone feeling attacked, ashamed, or isolated, it may weaken the very supports they rely on. That doesn't mean honesty was wrong – it may mean the way it was delivered needs rethinking.

Timing, Context, and Repair

If an honest conversation leads to distance, withdrawal, or rejection of support, don't assume the truth was the problem. Ask instead:

- Was the timing right?
- Was the context safe enough?
- Was the message clear and compassionate?

Sometimes the same truth needs a different moment, a calmer setting, or different people to be present. Sometimes, when emotions are running high, the most skilful move is to pause, breathe, and return to the conversation later with steadiness.

And sometimes, repair matters more than being right.

You can always say:

- *"I didn't say that as well as I wanted to."*
- *"I care about you – can we try that conversation again?"*

That, too, is honesty.

Honesty That Deepens Support

When done well, honest conversations don't weaken support – they deepen it. They bring relationships into a more real, grounded, and trustworthy place.

They say:

- *I care enough to be real with you.*
- *I trust you enough to tell the truth.*
- *I'm here – not to control you, but to care about your safety when you're struggling to protect yourself.*

This kind of honesty isn't easy. It takes courage and emotional skill. But it matters.

And when honesty is paired with genuinely caring, it becomes one of the most powerful forms of support there is.

Here's what I do:

1. **Make sure they feel understood and accepted first.**
   Listen. Give them time to talk so they feel heard and accepted.

2. **Be consistent in your support.**
   Show them you're for real – and that you're not going anywhere.

3. **Then be honest and truthful, in a thoughtful way.**

When I do this, I find that most of the time people appreciate the honesty and genuinely reflect on what I've said. I then help them process their thoughts around it by listening.

If they reject what I've said, I let it go. I thank them for listening. They have listened – and they have heard what I needed to say. They may think about it later. They may even bring it up at another time.

And be mindful, you can always return to the conversation – perhaps in a different context, or by expressing it in a slightly different way that they might be more open to, after you've both had time to reflect.

And be humble. You don't have all the answers, and you won't always know the best path forward. Sometimes the answers that seem right to you aren't actually the right ones for this situation. And sometimes the path that looks right isn't the right one for now – or isn't a good fit for them.

And sometimes it simply turns out not to be a helpful idea. We all have those from time to time. What matters is staying humble enough to recognise it, and willing to adjust when we do.

There are times I suggest an idea to a client that I genuinely believe in, we talk it through, and I realise it wasn't actually that good a suggestion. Sometimes I'll even say, "Well, that wasn't a very good idea I suggested – and I'm supposed to be the counsellor." We usually have a small chuckle about it, and then we move on.

More often than not, the best answers – and the best way forward – are the ones you figure out together.

Chapter Nine

What If They Don't Want to Change?

If they don't want to change, don't focus on change. Focus on engagement.

This is something people often get wrong. They assume progress only begins once someone wants to change. In reality, progress often starts long before that – sometimes without the words change or recovery ever being mentioned.

When I work with people who don't want to change, I don't talk to them about changing.

I don't push insight.
I don't argue with resistance.
I don't try to convince them of anything.

Instead, I keep it simple.

"How are you doing?"
"How was your week?"
"What do you want to work on today?"

That's it.

Often, they do have goals – just not the ones other people think they should have. I can listen to those. I can help them work towards what they care about.

Sometimes they don't believe they have a "problem" as such – but they know they're in distress and unhappy. They know something hurts. They know life isn't working the way it should. That's more than enough to begin.

So we talk about that.
How they see it.
What it's like for them.
What feels hard right now.

No pressure. No agenda.

And here's the quiet truth: engagement comes first. Change comes later – because someone engaged with them in a way that was meaningful to them.

When someone feels heard, respected, and not pushed, something softens. The conversation widens. Points of frustration and painful feelings are shared. Options can be reviewed. And steps toward change begin to develop naturally – maybe not addressing the addiction or mental-health concern directly – but change is happening.

So if they don't want to change, don't fight it.

Stay connected.
Stay curious.
Stay open.

That's where real movement starts.

I had a friend whose son was smoking heroin every day. She knew more about addiction than most – she had lived it herself – so they were able to talk openly about his use. He wasn't hiding from her. But he was clear about one thing: he didn't want to stop.

From the outside, his life still looked intact. He owned his own business. He was earning good money. He functioned. He was a little thin, but not enough to raise alarm. Most people would never have suspected he was using at all.

With his mother, though, he was honest – painfully so. He cried when he talked about it. He told her he used first thing in the morning, that he needed it just to function. He said heroin was almost always on his mind. Even when he was busy, even when he was doing other things, part of him was counting the hours, waiting for the next chance to get high again. He spoke about losing weight. He spoke about his lungs – the cough, the frequent chest infections that were starting to worry him.

She asked him if he would get support. He refused. He said he didn't want to stop. And she was left sitting with that unbearable helplessness – watching her son slowly disappear into something she recognised all too well.

When she told me all of this, the sadness in her was heavy. And I told her something that seemed, in that moment, to ease the weight she was carrying.

I told her not to focus on getting him to change his use.

Instead, I told her to focus on engagement, on connection.

To let him talk. To let him open up about his fears, his worries, his doubts – without pushing him toward decisions he wasn't ready to make. I suggested that, from time to time, she could gently mention options that existed if he ever wanted them – support for stopping, reducing, or simply being safer – and then ask what his concerns about those options might be. Not to persuade. Just to explore.

Even something as simple as encouraging him to see a doctor – not to change his use, but to check on his health – might be a step he could be open to.

Most importantly, I told her to let him know that support doesn't require commitment to change. That people are allowed to talk before they act. That even when someone isn't ready to stop, it still helps enormously to have a place where they can speak freely, process their feelings, and be understood. I told her that this is exactly what I do with clients – when they're not ready for change, that's okay. The talking itself matters. And quietly, almost invisibly, change often begins there without ever pushing for it.

By the end of our conversation, the reality of her son's addiction hadn't softened. The sadness was still there. But something else had appeared alongside it.

She felt relief.

She felt empowered to do something that was actually within her control – to stay connected, to stay open, to stay present. She felt she had permission to stop fighting for change before it was time. To let go of that burden. To trust the process of engagement – of human connection, of compassion, of a mother's healing love, a powerful force.

And that, for her, brought hope. A light we can hold in our hearts, for those who may have lost theirs.

Now let's consider a different situation.

Imagine a friend of yours has hoarding disorder, which is classified as a mental health condition. Over the years, you've watched their house slowly fill with items – piled up, blocking rooms, making it hard to move around, difficult to clean, and progressively interfering with their quality of life, reaching a critical point where daily life is no longer manageable.

From the outside, it's clear the situation is out of control. The environment is no longer hygienic. It has become unsafe and deeply problematic.

You've asked several times if they'd like help tidying the house a little. They even agreed. But when you start to work on it, they become visibly distressed at the idea of throwing anything away. The anxiety escalates. After a while, you stop, say "maybe another day", and leave it there.

So what now?

Rather than trying to force change, you decide not to push the hoarding itself.

Instead, you ask if they'd like to go for a walk together once a week – maybe in a nearby park. Fresh air. Movement. Time together, away from the house.

On these walks, they begin to talk about their life – current stresses, things on their mind, and sometimes the past, regrets and hurts that still linger. You might gently invite them to talk about how they feel about their home – not about changing it, just their thoughts on it. They may only share a few sentences. Don't push. Leave the space open, and another time they may talk about it again, as it begins to feel safe to do so.

In time, you might share some information about hoarding – not framed around fixing or changing it, but simply offering insight into how it develops and the kinds of supports that can help. They may find it interesting, perhaps even intriguing.

They may share that they've been feeling low. In truth, this is very likely, because whether they recognise it or not, the hoarding is having a profoundly detrimental impact on their wellbeing. You might suggest that they consider talking with a counsellor – not to address the hoarding directly, but to talk things through and explore how they're feeling.

That alone can be an important step forward – one of the many steps that will eventually lead them to a place where they can directly address their hoarding compulsion and recover from it.

You could share this book with them, suggesting they look at the progress-tracking tool in Chapter 3. Working with those questions doesn't require them to talk about, or work on, the hoarding problem at all – something that, at this point, is unlikely to be helpful to focus on.

If they say they're feeling low, you might say:

"It might help to look at these questions once a week and make a small plan for the week ahead."

This approach allows progress to begin without forcing conversations about hoarding before they are ready.

Each week, they could choose one small, achievable step in one or more of these areas:

- How did you do at connecting with positive and supportive people?

- How were things in your close relationships?

- How were things socially – at work, school, college, out shopping, or in groups you usually attend?

- How were your emotions and feelings?

- Overall, how was your week?

Before starting, you could ask how they feel about these questions. Let them know they can skip any they don't like or don't feel are relevant. They can also change how they answer – for example, using a 0–10 scale instead of the suggested options of *"difficult / not-so-good / OK"*, or choosing not to use a scale at all and simply talking the questions through.

This way, you're not focusing on something they're not ready to work on.

If you think about it, that's just being smart.

You're working through engagement – listening, presence, acceptance, and connection – and exploring areas they are open to working on.

And over time – when they are ready – the hoarding will likely enter the conversation naturally as something they may want to begin taking steps to address, perhaps small ones at first.

Here's the key: you're applying the same principle no matter the situation – helping them build recovery capital in a way that feels meaningful and right to them.

People move through different levels of awareness and readiness over time. Your role is not to force movement, but to meet them where they are — because that's how you have the greatest impact.

Levels of Awareness and Readiness

Below are some common levels of awareness and readiness you may encounter. These aren't steps to push someone through, but positions people may move between over time.

- **Not aware**
  They do not see any problem.

- **Aware of concerns**
  They sense that some things are not working well in their life, but do not see addiction or mental health as the issue.

- **Open to new perspectives**
  They are open to talking about and considering the possibility that substance use (or another addictive behaviour) or mental health may be part of the difficulty.

- **Beginning to recognise a concern**
  They believe they may have a mental health or addiction concern and are open to exploring how it might be addressed.

- **Aware and ready**
  They believe they have a mental health and/or addiction concern and are open to taking action.

- **Considering next steps**
  They are actively thinking about how to address their mental health and/or addiction concerns.

- **Actively taking steps – early stage**
  They are implementing a plan, learning new skills, and beginning the recovery journey.

- **Actively taking steps – middle stage**
  They have been working with a plan for some time – weeks or months – refining it, learning, and growing.

- **Actively taking steps – later stage**
  They are moving toward the later stages of recovery, consolidating progress and engaging well with supports.

- **Maintaining recovery**
  They are no longer in active addiction or struggling as they once were with a mental health con-

cern. Their focus is on sustaining their progress, with plans in place to manage lapses or relapses well should they occur, and to respond early to setbacks.

- **Embracing a new chapter**
  Recovery is no longer the central focus. They are building a meaningful life – pursuing goals, purpose, and wellbeing. They are now free to write the next chapter of their life.

Their Journey Is Not Linear

One week, someone may be hesitant even to consider that there is a problem, saying things like, *"It's really not that bad – things are actually OK."*
The next week, when you meet them again, they may have made a decision and be ready to take action, saying, *"OK, I'm ready to deal with this now."*

This happens. I've had clients arrive one week in a very different place from the week before – and that's where I meet them. When they say they're ready to act, I switch gears and say, *"OK, let's start looking at some steps we can talk through that you can take over the coming week to work on this."*

And they can start anywhere – at any level of awareness and readiness.

Sometimes people also move backwards. They may feel overwhelmed and need to step back – not to take active steps that week, but to pause, reflect, and review their options.

And you're there with them through all of it, adjusting your response as their relationship to the concern changes – meeting them at their current level of awareness and readiness, rather than insisting they stay where they were last week. Seeing it as a natural part of the process, not a setback or a failure.

Mismatching your approach to their level of awareness and readiness can feel frustrating for both of you.

If someone is only just beginning to consider that there may be a problem, and you are already encouraging plans and active steps, progress can stall and both parties may feel discouraged or stuck.

Equally, if they are ready to change and take action, but you remain focused only on exploring the concern, an important opportunity may be missed.

So take a step back. Ask yourself, *"What level of awareness and readiness are they at?"* Then ask, *"What's a good approach for me to take now?"*

Meeting someone where they are is the best way to help them move forward – to the next stage of their journey.

This might all sound very mechanical at first, or like a lot of conscious processing. But over time, it becomes natural – as you subtly switch gears to match where they are.

One day, you may even notice that within a single conversation they've moved from one level to another – and you've adjusted instinctively, without thinking about it at all.

Responding Well at Each Level of Awareness and Readiness

The best way to help someone move forward is to respond in a way that fits where they are right now.

Not aware

They do not see any problem.

Helpful responses:

- Stay connected.

- Ask neutral, everyday questions about how life is going.

- Explore how they see their life.

- Be present without trying to correct or persuade.

Aware of concerns

They sense something isn't working, but don't see addiction or mental health as the issue.

Helpful responses:

- Listen carefully to what feels difficult or frustrating for them.

- Explore how things affect their day-to-day life.

- Help them work on things they want to work on.

- Avoid linking concerns prematurely to addiction or mental health.

Open to new perspectives

They are open to considering that substance use or mental health may be part of the difficulty.

Helpful responses:

- Gently explore connections they raise themselves.

- Share information lightly, without labels, diagnosis or warnings.

- Ask curious questions rather than offering explanations.

- Normalise uncertainty and mixed feelings.

Beginning to recognise a concern

They believe there may be a mental health or addiction concern and are open to exploring it.

Helpful responses:

- Validate their insight and courage in naming it.

- Help them articulate what worries them most.

- Explore what is going on, without committing to action yet.

- Appreciate that understanding comes before change.

Aware and ready

They believe there is a concern and are open to taking action.

Helpful responses:

- Explore options, ask what kind of help or support feels right to them.

- Begin discussing possible next steps collaboratively.

- Keep goals small and flexible.

- Reassure them that they remain in control of decisions.

Considering next steps

They are actively thinking about how to address the concern.

Helpful responses:

- Help them weigh options without pushing a "right" choice.

- Talk through practical barriers and fears.

- Encourage one small, manageable step at a time.

- Frame action as experimentation, not commitment.

Actively taking steps – early stage

They are beginning to implement a plan.

Helpful responses:

- Support consistency rather than perfection.
- Help them review what helped and what didn't.
- Normalise uncertainty and doubt.
- Keep focus on effort, not outcomes.

Actively taking steps – middle stage

They have been working on recovery for a while now.

Helpful responses:

- Review progress regularly.
- Help refine strategies and supports.
- Watch for fatigue or discouragement.
- Encourage balance, not over-focus on recovery.

Actively taking steps – later stage

They are consolidating progress and moving toward stability.

Helpful responses:

- Shift focus toward sustaining progress.

- Strengthen routines, supports, and identity beyond recovery.

- Prepare for lapses without fear, knowing that they are not inevitable, but it's wise to have a sensible plan.

- Review the progress they have made and celebrate it.

Maintaining recovery

They are focused on sustaining wellbeing over time.

Helpful responses:

- Focus on balance and meaning in life.

- Help them notice early warning signs without alarm.

- Encourage ongoing reflection and self-care.

- Should they occur, treat lapses as opportunities for learning and growth, not failure.

Embracing a new chapter

Recovery is no longer central; life is opening up again.

Helpful responses:

- Support new goals, roles, and ambitions.

- Shift conversations toward purpose and fulfilment.

- Celebrate accomplishments and set new milestones for their life journey.

- Relate to them as a whole person, no longer primarily working on recovery with them.

A Simpler Appraoch

Sometimes, it helps to have a simple way, in the moment, to match your support to where they are. When you're unsure how to respond, ask yourself a few straightforward questions:

- Are they just beginning to awaken to an early awareness that something may not be right?

- Are they starting to recognise a problem and considering taking action?

- Are they actively taking steps to address a mental health and/or addiction concern?

- Have they recovered and are now focused on sustaining their progress and moving on to new goals?

Now, let's look a little closer at each one.

1. Early awareness is just beginning

They may only have a vague sense that something isn't quite right.

Helpful ways to respond:

Stay connected and emotionally available

Ask gentle, everyday questions about how life is going

Listen without trying to interpret or explain

Reflect back what you hear, without adding conclusions

Let them talk themselves into clarity, in their own time

At this stage, presence matters more than insight.

2. Recognising a problem and considering action

They can now name a difficulty, but may feel unsure, conflicted, or overwhelmed.

Helpful ways to respond:

Acknowledge the courage it takes to say something isn't working

Help them clarify what feels most concerning or disruptive

Explore what they've already tried, and what helped even a little

Ask what kind of support feels useful right now

Avoid rushing toward solutions or commitments

Understanding comes before change.

3. Taking action

They are actively doing something — seeking support, changing habits, or trying new strategies.

Helpful ways to respond:

Encourage small, manageable steps rather than big goals

Focus on effort and learning, not success or failure

Help them notice what's helping and what's not

Normalise doubt, wobble, and mixed feelings

Reinforce that they remain in control of decisions

Progress is rarely linear — and that's normal.

4. Sustaining progress and moving on

Recovery is no longer the centre of life; wellbeing and meaning are coming back into focus.

Helpful ways to respond:

Shift conversations toward balance, purpose, and future goals

Support routines that sustain wellbeing without over-monitoring

Treat lapses, if they occur, as information — not failure

Celebrate progress and acknowledge how far they've come

Relate to them as a whole person, not someone "in recovery"

The goal is a full life — not lifelong management.

Most important, be yourself. You have a natural ability to engage with people in ways that feel right. Let it flow. Trust in your qualities — humour, compassion, and tact.

The most important thing is that you are there and that you care. More than anything, that's what matters to people when they are struggling. And that's what they remember when they have recovered.

You Don't Need to Push Change for Change to Happen

When you meet someone where they are, stay connected, and respond in a way that fits their current level of awareness and readiness, progress unfolds naturally. Sometimes slowly. Sometimes unevenly. Sometimes in ways you don't immediately notice.

But over time, these moments of attunement add up. Trust grows. Conversations widen. And when the moment for change arrives, it doesn't feel forced – it feels right.

Meeting someone where they are is the best way to help them move forward – to the next stage of their journey.

Change emerges through connection.
Opportunities for change are always present – it is always possible.

In fact, if you take time to notice, change is always happening.

Chapter Ten

The Greatest Secret of Recovery

If there's one thing to take from this book, it's this:

You don't need to fix anyone.
You don't need perfect words.
You don't need to carry their recovery on your shoulders.

What helps most is steadiness.

Being present.
Being genuine.
Being honest.

HELP A FRIEND RECOVER

Knowing when to speak, when to listen, and when to step back.

Recovery rarely unfolds in straight lines. There will be progress, setbacks, pauses, and moments of uncertainty. That's not failure – it's how change actually happens. Your role is not to force the outcome, but to remain a calm, reliable presence as things unfold.

Sometimes what you say will land.
Sometimes it won't – yet.
Sometimes your concern will be heard long before it's acted on.

That's okay.

You're adding support, not controlling the process.
You're contributing, not rescuing.
And that matters more than you may ever fully see.

Think about how you would feel going through a difficult time – with a friend who is steady, wise, and committed to supporting you. Someone who grows alongside you, stays present, and offers what they can to the process. That kind of support matters more than we often realise.

Remember to protect your own safety and wellbeing. Stay connected to support for yourself. Pace yourself. You're far more helpful when you're grounded, rested, and clear.

And finally, trust this:

Care offered with honesty, compassion, and respect is never wasted. Even when change is slow, even when things feel uncertain, your presence can be one of the most stabilising forces in someone's life.

You're not meant to do this perfectly.
You're meant to do it humanly.

And that is enough.

Stay steady. You're doing better than you think.

And here is the greatest secret of it all: Recovery is joyful.

I've been doing this work for over twenty years. From time to time, clients ask me, "How do you keep going?" They assume I must be exhausted by it all – worn down or burnt out. But the opposite is true. I love this work.

Seeing people move from despair to hope, from unbearable pain to feeling comforted, from isolation to knowing they are not alone – and being alongside them on their journey – is a wonderful and deeply moving experience. Even changing me as a person.

And soon, you will know how joyful it is to walk alongside someone you care deeply about see them recover. It is truly a life changing experience.

After more than twenty years of doing this work, this is what I've learned – a truth that keeps me grounded, happy, and able to give my best to the people I support. A mantra I return to whenever I struggle in the process of helping another heal:

> *"I can't save, fix, or cure anyone – but I can always humbly add to their recovery capital, often in many ways."*

I hope that as you reach out to support those you care about, this wisdom crosses your mind from time to time – illuminating the way.

Ongoing Support & Next Steps

Your journey doesn't end here.

Visit **www.WellbeingTrackers.com** to download The Recovery Tracker and book a free consultation with the author.

Website details correct at the time of publication.

About the Author

Gearóid Carey has spent over 20 years helping people recover from addiction, trauma, and mental health challenges. With a master's degree in counselling, he has worked across diverse settings – guiding people from crisis to stability and beyond. His mission: to make recovery simpler and achievable for everyone.

Discover More Books

- Recovery Made Simple: Two Steps to Heal Your Life

- WB-48: The Total Wellbeing Programme – Live Beyond Your Dreams

- 50 Years of Research and the End of the Mental Health Industrial Complex

- Counselling Made Simple

- How to Create Self-Tracking Tools

- 2-Step Recovery Services

- A Completed Model of the Human Species

- The Monsters Among Us
- The Standard Enlightened Diet
- Creative Solutions to Economic Problems
- Territory
- Journey to Democracy
- Blissful Sex & Relationships: A Guide for Men
- I Woke from a Dream
- The Technology That Will Save Us All

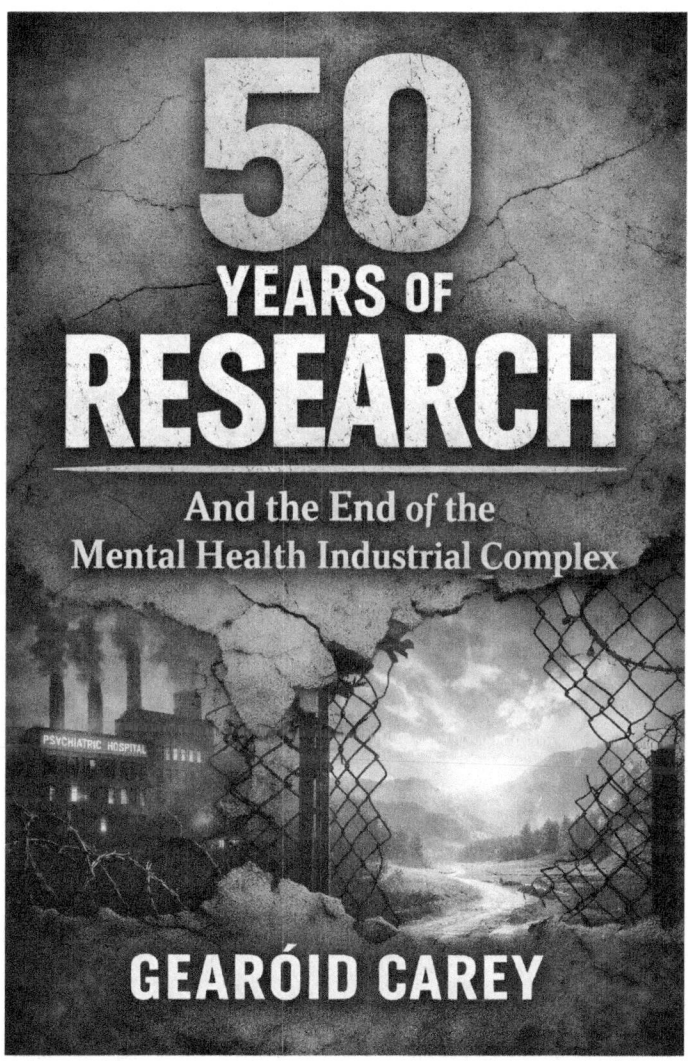

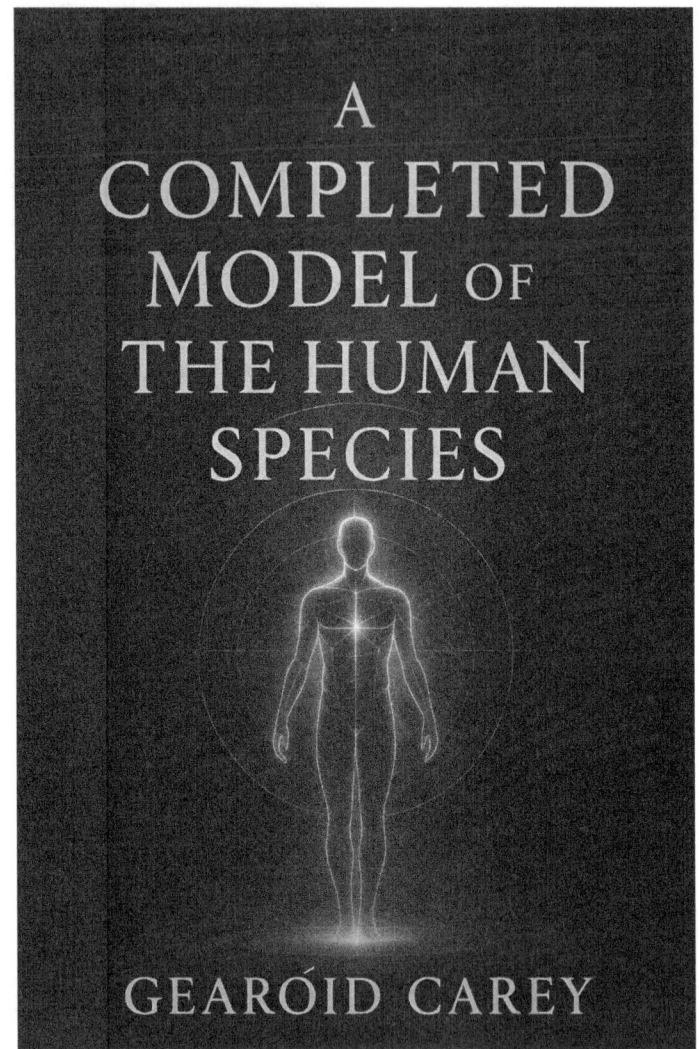

THE STANDARD ENLIGHTENED DIET

The Art of Living in Harmony
Through Enlightened Eating

GEARÓID CAREY

Printed in Dunstable, United Kingdom